NEWLY COMMISSIONED NAVAL OFFICER'S GUIDE

Second Edition

TITLES IN THE SERIES

The Bluejacket's Manual
Career Compass
The Chief Petty Officer's Guide
Command at Sea
Dictionary of Modern Strategy and Tactics
Dictionary of Naval Abbreviations
Dictionary of Naval Terms
Division Officer's Guide
Dutton's Nautical Navigation
Farwell's Rules of the Nautical Road
Fleet Tactics and Naval Operations
International Law for Seagoing Officers
Naval Ceremonies, Customs, and Traditions
The Naval Institute Guide to Naval Writing
The Naval Officer's Guide
Naval Shiphandler's Guide
Newly Commissioned Naval Officer's Guide
Operations Officer's Guide
Principles of Naval Engineering
Principles of Naval Weapon Systems
The Professional Naval Officer: A Course to Steer By
Reef Points
A Sailor's History of the U.S. Navy
Saltwater Leadership
Shiphandling Fundamentals for Littoral Combat Ships and the New Frigates
Watch Officer's Guide

THE U.S. NAVAL INSTITUTE
Blue & Gold Professional Library

For more than one hundred years, U.S. Navy professionals have counted on specialized books published by the Naval Institute Press to prepare them for their responsibilities as they advance in their careers and to serve as ready references and refreshers when needed. From the days of coal-fired battleships to the era of unmanned aerial vehicles and laser weaponry, such perennials as *The Bluejacket's Manual* and the *Watch Officer's Guide* have guided generations of sailors through the complex challenges of naval service. As these books are updated and new ones are added to the list, they will carry the distinctive mark of the Blue & Gold Professional Library series to remind and reassure their users that they have been prepared by naval professionals and meet the exacting standards that sailors have long expected from the U.S. Naval Institute.

11/29/18

Brandon,

Deepest thanks for being the ultimate shipmate at SHAPE! From cookies to exabyte comms, you've been an ace and I'd serve with you anywhere, anytime!

NEWLY COMMISSIONED NAVAL OFFICER'S GUIDE

Second Edition

RDML Fred W. Kacher, USN

NAVAL INSTITUTE PRESS
Annapolis, Maryland

Naval Institute Press
291 Wood Road
Annapolis, MD 21402

© 2018 by the United States Naval Institute
All rights reserved. No part of this book may be reproduced or utilized in any form or by any means, electronic or mechanical, including photocopying and recording, or by any information storage and retrieval system, without permission in writing from the publisher.

Library of Congress Cataloging-in-Publication Data
Names: Kacher, Fred W, author.
Title: Newly commissioned naval officer's guide / RDML Fred W. Kacher, USN.
Description: 2nd edition. | Annapolis, Maryland : Naval Institute Press, [2018]
 | Series: The U.S. Naval Institute blue & gold professional library | Includes bibliographical references and index.
Identifiers: LCCN 2018013319 | ISBN 9781682473658 (pbk. : alk. paper)
Subjects: LCSH: United States. Navy—Officers' handbooks. | United States. Navy—Military life—Handbooks, manuals, etc.
Classification: LCC V133 .K33 2018 | DDC 359.00973—dc23
LC record available at https://lccn.loc.gov/2018013319

♾ Print editions meet the requirements of ANSI/NISO z39.48-1992 (Permanence of Paper).
Printed in the United States of America.

26 25 24 23 22 21 20 19 18   9 8 7 6 5 4 3 2 1
First printing

Contents

	List of Illustrations	ix
	Preface	xi
	List of Abbreviations	xv
	Introduction	1
1	Leadership: The Core of What We Do	3
2	Your First Duty	14
3	Naval Customs	31
4	Social Etiquette	41
5	Leave, Liberty, and Travel	51
6	Pay and Benefits	60
7	Understanding U.S. Navy Programs and Policies	69
8	Naval Correspondence and Administration	84
9	Managing Your Career	96
10	Advice for Navy Spouses	112
11	Basic Naval Management	124
12	Getting the Most out of Naval Schools	139
13	Voices of Command	152
	Appendix 1 *Overview of the History of the U.S. Navy*	163
	Appendix 2 *Useful Websites*	171
	Appendix 3 *The Chief of Naval Operations Professional Reading Program . . . and Beyond*	177
	Index	185

Illustrations

Photos

The journey begins	xx
Leadership opportunities arise in many forms in the Navy	11
Even in your first job you will be making a difference	15
Honors and ceremonies are an integral part of the Navy's heritage	37
A wetting-down ceremony celebrates an officer's promotion	43
ENS James Zumwalt makes a drawing for a child in an orphanage in Vietnam	53
The Navy invests in its people and their families through a variety of benefits	66
The Navy is committed to creating an environment in which every leader can excel and grow	70
An ensign gives a safety brief prior to a crash-and-salvage drill	88
A strong operational performance will factor prominently in your selection for leadership responsibilities	99
For more than two hundred years, homecomings have been special for the Navy and our families	122
An ensign relays information during a training exercise	129
Members of a BUD/S class participate in intensive physical training	142
The commanding officer is the most senior mentor on the ship	154

~ ix ~

Figures

1-1	Helpful Hints: What Is Expected of You—A Quick Tip	10
2-1	Sample Orders	17
11-1	Sample Correspondence	127
12-1	Helpful Hints: How Naval Schools Are Different from College	140

Preface

Like most endeavors related to the U.S. Navy, this book is the product of a multitude of naval leaders working together. Over the years, the *Newly Commissioned Naval Officer's Guide* has taken several forms, but all have conveyed the deep desire to help incoming generations of young naval officers entering the fleet. This second edition of this book's current form owes a deep debt to the authors who wrote those previous editions.

As this new generation of ensigns "hits the fleet," they report to a Navy that is rising to challenges both traditional and transformational. Since this book's last inception, the emergence of information technology, the broader integration of women into the Navy, the attacks on 11 September 2001, and ensuing conflicts in Iraq and Afghanistan have all demonstrated that the naval service is an evolving profession, and the return to Great Power competition proves that this current decade is no exception. At the same time, many of the Navy's attributes and challenges remain as eternal as the sea, and ensigns of previous generations will still recognize many of the challenges that our new ensigns face today.

With this book I have attempted to provide aspiring leaders with some of the benefits of a personal mentor. Because my experiences as a young ensign occurred some time ago, it was clear to me that the perspective of those who served more recently as ensigns would be essential. I have been fortunate to benefit from the insight and talent of some extraordinary junior officers whose experiences as newly commissioned officers were much more recent than mine—this book would not have been possible without their help.

LCDR Sam O'Neil, a wonderful leader and writer, served as the main driver of the current edition during times when my professional duties precluded my giving this project the attention it required. I also thank LCDR Rob Keller, LT Anthony Lichi, and LT Marissa Legg, terrific officers all, who reviewed a number of the chapters from this book's previous edition and not only made those chapters better but made them their own. Our efforts, of course, stand on the shoulders of those who played such an essential role in the 2009 edition, to include LCDR Jim Rushton, J'aime Rushton, Sara Green, CAPT T. J. Zerr, and LCDR John Liddle. Finally, I thank CDR Micah Murphy, CDR Rob Niemeyer, and Sam O'Neil for their work in bringing the Navy's reading program alive for this book as well as compiling a useful website list that genuinely reflects what young ensigns rely on in the fleet.

As I reflect on my own experience as an ensign, I would also like to thank CAPT Steve Lehr, USN (Ret.), CAPT Rick Wright, USN (Ret.), and CAPT Andy Pitts, USN (Ret.), who loomed very large in my life as my commanding officers during my days as a young junior officer. I would also like to acknowledge CAPT Jake Ross, USN (Ret.) and CAPT Joe Corsi, USN (Ret.), who were both extraordinary mentors as I started to lead ensigns for the first time as a department head. Finally, I thank CAPT Terry Culton, CAPT Chip Denman, and CAPT Jeff Wolstenholme, my commanding officers when I served as their executive officer; USS *Barry*'s record during your respective command tours looks even more impressive and admirable now that I have had command myself.

I am grateful to have worked for some senior leaders who were never too busy to share their insights and mentorship: ADM Mike Mullen, USN (Ret.), ADM James Stavridis, USN (Ret.), ADM Phil Davidson, VADM John Morgan, USN (Ret.), VADM Doug Crowder, USN (Ret.), VADM Pete Daly, USN (Ret.), VADM Tom Rowden, USN (Ret.), RADM Ron Boxall, and CAPT Gerry Roncolato, USN (Ret.). Additionally, I thank Bryan McGrath, Vince McBeth, and Todd Leavitt, three extraordinary leaders just a few years senior to me who served as powerful role models and whose crews were honored to call them captain.

Just as leadership is essential in the fleet, it is also important in the production of a book. LCDR Tom Cutler, USN (Ret.) has served as a superb coach, and his dedication to the naval service—both in uniform and in his current role at USNI—are without peer. Having been a complete novice in this process when I led the development of the first edition, I could not have asked for a better mentor or role model. In this second edition, I thank Jim Dolbow for his superb mentorship as well.

Lastly, I would like to thank my family for their support. My wife, Pam, has always been willing to read and reflect on my writing despite being an incredibly busy and dedicated wife and mother of my two daughters, Jen and Katie, who have perhaps had to sacrifice the most as I worked in a profession that I have loved. I also thank my parents, Fred and Nancy Kacher, for serving as the original examples of leadership and patriotism in my life.

Leading as a new junior officer is both an art and a science. In some ways ensigns are asked to do the improbable—lead with confidence and skill Sailors who are often older and more experienced than they are. Yet every generation of ensigns has managed not only to survive but also to thrive in their roles as front-line leaders in the world's greatest Navy. This book is dedicated to these young leaders—past, present, and future—who by their service make a difference in our Navy, our nation, and the world.

Abbreviations

3M	maintenance, material, and management system
AMC	Air Mobility Command
API	aviation preflight indoctrination
ARI	alcohol-related incident
ASW	antisubmarine warfare
ATRC	Aegis Training and Readiness Center
BAH	basic allowance for housing
BAS	basic allowance for subsistence
BCA	body composition assessment
BOL	BUPERS Online
BRS	Blended Retirement System
BUD/S	basic underwater demolition
BUPERS	Bureau of Naval Personnel
CAC	common access card
CAS	collaboration at sea
CBQ	combined bachelor's quarters
CDO	command duty officer
CEC	Civil Engineer Corps
CECOS	Civil Engineer Corps Officer School
CFC	Combined Federal Campaign
CFL	command fitness leader

CFS	command financial specialist
CIA	controlled industrial area
CIC	combat information center
CICWO	combat information center watch officer
CMC	command master chief
CMEO	command managed equal opportunity
CNO	Chief of Naval Operations
CNO PRP	Chief of Naval Operations Professional Reading Program
CO	commanding officer
COMREL	community relations
CPO	chief petty officer
CWO	chief warrant officer
DAPA	drug and alcohol prevention adviser
DFAS	Defense Finance Accounting Service
DIMs	daily intention messages
DINFOS	Defense Information School
DITS	Division in the Spotlight
DoD	Department of Defense
DOSP	division officer sequencing plan
ED	engineering duty
EDA	expected date of arrival
EDD	expected detachment date
EDO	engineering duty officer
EO	Equal Opportunity program
EOD	explosive ordnance officer
EOOW	engineering officer of the watch
FAO	foreign area officer
FAP	Family Advocacy Program
FCP	Family Care Plan
FFSC	Fleet and Family Support Center
FISC	Fleet Industrial Supply Center
FITREP	fitness report
FSA	family separation allowance
FST	full-time support officer

FTS	full-time support
HMO	health maintenance organization
HR	human resource
IO	intelligence officer
IP	information professional officer
IW	information warfare officer
JAG	judge advocate general
JCCS	Joint Crew Composite Squadron
JFTR	Joint Federal Travel Regulations
JO	junior officer
JOSN	journalist seaman
JPME	joint professional military education
LCPO	leading chief petty officer
LDO	limited duty officer
LES	leave and earnings statement
LPO	leading petty officer
MCPON	Master Chief Petty Officer of the Navy
MEB	medical evaluation board
MNP	My Navy Portal
MSFD	main space fire doctrine
MTF	military treatment facility
MWR	morale, welfare, and recreation
NATOPS	naval air training and operating procedures standards
NAVSUP	Naval Supply Systems Command
NFO	naval flight officer
NJP	nonjudicial punishment
NPC	Navy Personnel Command
NPRP	Navy Professional Reading Program
NPS	Naval Postgraduate School
NROTC	Naval Reserve Officers Training Corps
NSIPS	Navy Standard Integrated Personnel System
NWU	Navy working uniform
OCE	officer conducting the exercise
OCS	Officer Candidate School

ODC	officer data card
OMPF	official military personnel file
OOD	officer of the deck
OPSEC	operational security
OSR	officer service record
OTC	officer in tactical command
PAO	public affairs officer
PCS	permanent change of station
PFA	physical fitness assessment
PLR	PSD liaison representative
POA&M	plan of action and milestones
POD	plan of the day
PQS	personnel qualification standards
PRD	planned rotation date
PRT	physical readiness test
PSD	personnel support detachment
PSR	performance summary record
PT	physical training
ROTC	Reserve Officers' Training Corps
SAPR	Sexual Assault Prevention and Response program
SEAL	sea-air-land
SGLI	Servicemembers' Group Life Insurance
SHIPSUP	shipbuilding superintendent
SLA	special leave accrual
SNA	student naval aviator
SOBC	Submarine Officer Basic Course
SOES	SGLI Online Enrollment System
SWO	surface warfare officer
SWSCO	surface warfare supply corps officer
TA	tuition assistance
TAD	temporary additional duty
TAO	tactical action officer
TDY	temporary duty
TPU	Transient Personnel Unit

TSP	Thrift Savings Plan
UCMJ	Uniform Code of Military Justice
URL	unrestricted line officer
VA	victim advocate
WCS	work center supervisor
XO	executive officer
XOI	Executive Officer Inquiry

The journey begins . . .
U.S. Navy, Shannon O'Connor

Introduction

For newly commissioned U.S. Navy officers opening this book, congratulations as you begin a new chapter in your life. You have embarked on a journey of consequence and purpose that will stay with you forever, regardless of the path the rest of your life takes.

While no book can substitute for a great personal mentor, this book focuses on the very things a good mentor would pass on to you. As you read the advice in this book, be mindful that the path to success for a newly commissioned officer is not a political tightrope on which you must avoid risk to survive and advance. Instead, take comfort that your leaders will expect you to learn and grow and that no ensign in history has completely avoided making a mistake. Far more important than avoiding mistakes is the importance of taking action. Most naval leaders would prefer to have someone working for them who does ninety-five things out of one hundred correctly rather than someone who does only ten things perfectly in the same period of time. Planning, study, and practice will help you minimize mistakes (and avoid repeating earlier ones), but above all else your leaders expect you to listen, lead, learn, and take action.

As you begin this life of action and leadership, you will quickly find that there are very few "silver bullet" solutions in life or in the Navy. Hard work, respect for your people, and staying positive are just a few of the traits that will always be prized in the Navy and other high-demand, high-reward organizations. Cramming for the test the night before rarely succeeds in life or in the

Navy. As in sports, success in the U.S. Navy will be the product of preparation, repetition, and effort that occur long before game day. You will see this principle reflected throughout this book: tomorrow's success depends on your hard work and preparation today.

Leaders at your commissioning source likely emphasized that accountability is the bedrock of our profession; your early experiences in the Navy will drive home this point vividly. Smooth talk and subject matter expertise will not compensate for failure to achieve results. You will find that this spirit of results, not excuses, permeates our service and is the watchword of the Sailors who will work for you. Because of this, the U.S. Navy is as close to a true meritocracy as we have in our society. Excellence and hard work will always serve you well.

An old adage says, "The most important job you'll ever have is the one you have today." This is great advice no matter where you serve. Regardless of your long-term goal—or the desirability of your new assignment—if you focus your effort and talents on the job at hand, future opportunities will often fall into place. There is nothing wrong with planning for your future and aiming for long-term goals, but first you must be committed to give your very best to your current job.

Many former junior officers—whether they are admirals, chief executive officers, or are among the seven presidents who have served as naval officers—look back at their early commissioned service as some of the most satisfying years of their lives. Of course, few things worth doing come without hard work, and the life of a junior officer is one of both great opportunity and great challenge. The goal of this book is to provide the insights and tips for success that will help you make this journey a successful one. Welcome aboard!

1

Leadership
The Core of What We Do

Regardless of whether you have been commissioned with plans to serve as a SEAL or in the Supply Corps, as an officer in the U.S. Navy you will be expected to be a leader. As you begin training pipelines that are designed to equip you with the expertise and skills to perform your first duty assignment, you should never lose sight of this fact. Soon many of you will be placed in charge of Sailors who will be expecting you to provide their course for the day and direction for their organization.

This first leadership opportunity can be both exhilarating and a bit intimidating, and both feelings are understandable. Very much like preparing for a big game or performance, it would be surprising if you did not feel a few butterflies before starting your first job. The good news is that your training and the qualities that earned you a commission will help you to follow in the footsteps of the generations of ensigns who have gone before you.

While leaders come in many shapes, sizes, and styles, following a few general principles will equip you well for your first year as an officer in the Navy. Whether you will be in a training pipeline for quite some time after your commission or you expect to lead Sailors fairly soon, these guidelines on leadership and personal behavior will help you succeed in the fleet.

Lead by Example

At first it may seem surprising that a new ensign is expected to lead or provide an example for more experienced troops, but that is exactly the case. In the very early stages at your first command, leading by example will largely focus on doing correct things on an individual scale, such as staying fit, wearing a good uniform, and carrying yourself in a positive and businesslike manner. However, your ability to lead by example will soon expand to include a focus on operational proficiency, efficient correspondence, and a demonstrated commitment to both your command and your Sailors.

Be Early

From our very first days at school we have been taught to be punctual, so this advice may seem obvious. The demand for you to be on time becomes much more profound when your Sailors and your chain of command are also depending on your timeliness. Just as important, your commitment to be on time signals to those who lead you and to those you will lead that you respect their time and that they should respect yours. For many of you, real-world operational requirements will depend upon you and your subordinates being ready and on time to perform your mission.

Be Yourself

Demonstrate the positive qualities that ensured your success prior to entering the Navy. Being yourself does not imply that you "let it all hang out" by advertising your weaknesses. Instead, aspire to be your best self in a natural and authentic manner by working modestly on your weaknesses and playing to your strengths. Do not pretend to be something you are not. If you are naturally a bit reserved or measured, do not try to be the loud cheerleader; you will not look comfortable, and Sailors will know when you are faking it. Instead, allow yourself to grow into your role.

Command Your Organization

Whether you are leading a traditional division on a submarine or ship or managing in an office environment, your leaders and your Sailors are going to expect you to take charge. Your Sailors will want to see you making decisions, leading evolutions, and showing interest in them and their work. Some new ensigns very quickly take to their leadership role, but you may find it a bit uncomfortable to step into this role without having gained comprehensive knowledge in your field. Although you will want to do everything you can to prepare to lead in your respective service community, you will find that in the Navy as in life, you will rarely have perfect information to make a decision or take the lead on a project. Leading in the Navy involves managing risk, dealing with unknowns, and stepping up to your leadership role.

Focus on Warfighting and Operational Competence

The U.S. Navy is an operational fighting force, so the majority of newly commissioned officers will be assigned to an operational job, whether it is flying an aircraft, driving a ship, or participating in ground missions. In many cases you will quickly be expected to lead your Sailors while conducting tactical operations or efforts that support combat operations. More broadly, your Sailors may look to you for guidance and information on the Navy's larger roles, missions, and policies, so be ready to dedicate yourself to becoming an eternal student of the naval profession by honoring your craft every day.

Set the Standard

Whether you are conducting a daily cleanliness assessment of your workspaces, evaluating written reports, or leading a debrief of a tactical evolution, you will have many opportunities to signal your standards to your Sailors. Although some Sailors will always exceed your expectations, most will perform to the standards you set. If you accept unclean spaces, poorly written reports, or hastily executed drills, this is what you will continue to see. If, conversely, you highlight the things you and your team need to work on and provide the team the opportunity to practice and train, you will almost certainly be rewarded with improved performance. Never walk past a problem; this will signal that you tacitly approve of the issue you ignored. Even if you are in a hurry, take a moment to point out the problem to a responsible Sailor in the space or write down the issue so you can discuss it with your senior enlisted leaders at a more opportune time.

Be Prepared to Deliver the Hard News

Whether you are debriefing your boss or providing feedback to your Sailors, you must have the courage to deliver the unvarnished truth. There will inevitably come a time when you must tell your team that their results did not match expectations or tell your commanding officer that something is not going well.

Giving negative feedback is not often in vogue, but being able to criticize tactfully and constructively and to correct weaknesses will be necessary to move your people and your organization forward. Few people enjoy criticism, but providing clear, honest feedback as early as possible will prevent tougher situations in the future.

Show Integrity

You will be expected to choose the hard right over the easy wrong every time. Your assurance that a job has been completed or that a maintenance check is satisfactory must be ironclad, and lives will depend on your commitment to do the right thing. The sea is an inherently dangerous environment, and there is no place on a ship or in our profession for someone who cannot be trusted to tell the truth regardless of the consequences. Your word must be your bond.

Be Courageous

For some ensigns, particularly those in the special warfare and aviation communities, courage in the face of physical risks will be required on an early and regular basis. Those in other communities may be assigned rewarding but hazardous duties such as serving maritime interception teams or on the ground in Iraq or Afghanistan that will also challenge them to show courage. Every ensign, however, should be committed to show courage as a leader, courage as a human being, and courage to do the right thing.

Focus on Your Sailors

Although you are a new ensign, one job that starts right away is your duty to lead and care for the Sailors under your leadership. The paradigm of leading the whole person may seem intrusive compared with civilian occupations in which concern for employees usually ends when they depart their workplace. Everything from your Sailors' pay to their professional development is part of your leadership portfolio. This does not mean that you will be able to approve every special request or leave chit that crosses your desk, but it is your job to support your Sailors so they can take care of the mission.

Find a way to learn each Sailor's face, rank, and last name along with his or her family situation and goals. Divisions at sea will have a division officer's notebook that contains this information. Even if you are not in an environment where a division officer notebook is in place or practical, there are a number of ways to ensure that you have command of the details of your Sailors' lives. Some leaders have had their Sailors fill out index cards with relevant personal information that can be reviewed easily; computers and smartphones offer more modern and convenient ways to store this information.

Practice Management by Walking Around

One of the simplest ways of getting to know your Sailors, their jobs, and your equipment is by walking around. Really. Get out of your office, engage your Sailors, and ask them questions. It is easy to get bogged down by administrative tasks, and you can find yourself sitting in front of a computer all day. In some cases you might require the use of a computer located in your stateroom or an office that is separate from where your Sailors work. Even if you are working on something important, consistently spending large portions of the day working away from your Sailors is not sustainable leadership in the Navy. Instead, walk around; it will likely make you fresher when you return to your desk, and it will also better enable you to assess the culture and the climate of your division while demonstrating your interest in what your Sailors do and who they are.

Respect and Humility Go a Long Way

You may outrank your enlisted personnel, but you will need to respect them and rely on their expertise if you are to succeed. Put another way, talent and knowledge are not always commensurate with rank. In certain areas of naval life, junior Sailors who are working most closely with their equipment and performing day-to-day tasks may be the most likely people to provide solutions to some of the challenges your division or office faces.

Learn to Plan

Hope is not a strategy. As you progress as a leader, planning for broader operational challenges and for the future will become a key competency. While the uninitiated might think that planning and scheduling are for naval leaders more senior than a new ensign, that is not the case. You will be asked to plan and lead projects or operational evolutions in fairly short order. This opportunity to plan and oversee the execution of your efforts is one of the great opportunities that make our naval profession so special. Much like professional sports coaches who spend many more hours preparing their team for the game than the actual time it takes to play it, you will often find that your efforts to plan an evolution will far exceed the time it takes to actually carry it out.

Remembering a few basics of naval planning will help you with this endeavor. First, recognize that references and examples are available to guide you in your planning and execution for most of the challenges you will face. Second, you will often have department heads and senior enlisted people to help you in the planning process. Finally, remember that planning almost always takes longer than you think it will, so start the planning process early. Ultimately, by planning with attention to detail and with ample time, you and your team will have a sense of confidence as you begin to execute your plan.

Look Forward

Great leaders look beyond their in-boxes. Most of your Sailors will be focused on completing the immediate tasks before them, and rightfully so. As their leader, with the help of your department head and senior enlisted leadership partner, you will be expected to think beyond the day-to-day. Whether it is creating a plan to help your Sailors get selected for promotion or creating more opportunities to hone their tactical skills, you must always be looking ahead.

Listen to Your Senior Enlisted Leadership Partners

In most working situations that you will encounter, your principal leadership partner will be a chief petty officer (CPO) or leading petty officer (LPO). These senior enlisted leaders will be particularly valuable partners during your first few months at your new command. These relationships will evolve as you develop confidence and begin making broader decisions. This progression is healthy and expected, but you should work hard to maintain positive relationships with your senior enlisted leadership as your own skills increase. This does not mean that you should always defer to them, and in rare cases you may have to deal with chiefs who are not performing well, but the poorly performing chief is by far the exception, not the rule.

Be a Good Follower

In addition to being strong leader, it is just as important for you to be a good follower. As you lead, you will execute the visions and policies of your commanding officer and your department heads, and you will support broader naval policy in general. You will often be the person who articulates these policies and directives to your Sailors.

There may be times when you will not agree with the policies or plans you are being asked to support. There is a long-standing tradition of loyal dissent in the Navy, but this dissent must end when your leaders transition from deliberating a course of action to executing this decision. Your seniors will be counting on you to bring their policies to life with honor, courage, and commitment—the Navy's core values—just as you expect your own subordinates to support your decisions. Think of being a good follower in terms of the Golden Rule: follow your leaders as you want your subordinates to follow you.

If the Navy Is New for You

The prior enlisted person who has just received a commission is already familiar with the Navy's service and business cultures. For new ensigns starting their first full-time naval job after commissioning, though, it is worth touching on some basic tenets of naval culture that may not have been obvious from summer training and cruises. Not all of these observations are intrinsically related to the topic of leadership, but understanding these cultural touchstones will help you lead more effectively:

You Are No Longer Living in a Nine-to-Five World

The Navy and the other armed services operate around the world twenty-four hours a day, seven days a week. The importance of their work and the excitement of real-world operations provide a vibrancy and variety that many career naval officers love. Operational considerations as varied as what time high tide occurs in a channel to the moonlight needed to complete a night ground mission may require that your workdays begin very early or end very late relative to those of other professions—and those workdays will not always fall between Monday and Friday.

The Navy Starts Early

While the military's focus on getting an early start on the day is well known, a surprising number of new officers have struggled with the early starting times of the day. If you are on a ship, reveille usually occurs at 0600 on the weekdays, even if you are in port, and most shore commands begin their days between 0700 and 0800—an hour or more earlier than the average civilian workplace.

Figure 1-1
Helpful Hints: What Is Expected of You—A Quick Tip

Besides many of the obvious attributes that make a naval career so interesting and exciting, one of the benefits of working in a very mature organization is that there are usually well-articulated expectations and benchmarks to guide your performance. In this case, the fitness reports that your seniors will use to evaluate your performance include seven traits:

Professional expertise
Professional knowledge, proficiency, and qualifications.

Command or organizational climate/equal opportunity
Contributing to growth and development, human worth, community.

Military bearing/character
Appearance, conduct, physical fitness, adherence to Navy core values.

Teamwork
Contributions toward team building and team results.

Mission accomplishment and initiative
Taking initiative, planning/prioritizing, achieving mission.

Leadership
Organizing, motivating, and developing others to accomplish goals.

Tactical Performance (warfare-qualified officers only)
Basic and tactical employment of weapons systems.

While good fitness reports should be the by-product of great performance and not the driving force behind it, these seven attributes will always be expected of you.

Timeliness Is a Core Virtue

Although we discussed punctuality earlier in this chapter, it warrants additional mention for those who have had limited exposure to the Navy. Because so many more people will be counting on you to be where you need to be on time, you will find that timeliness has never been more important. It is very common in Navy meetings to observe those with experience arriving five to ten minutes

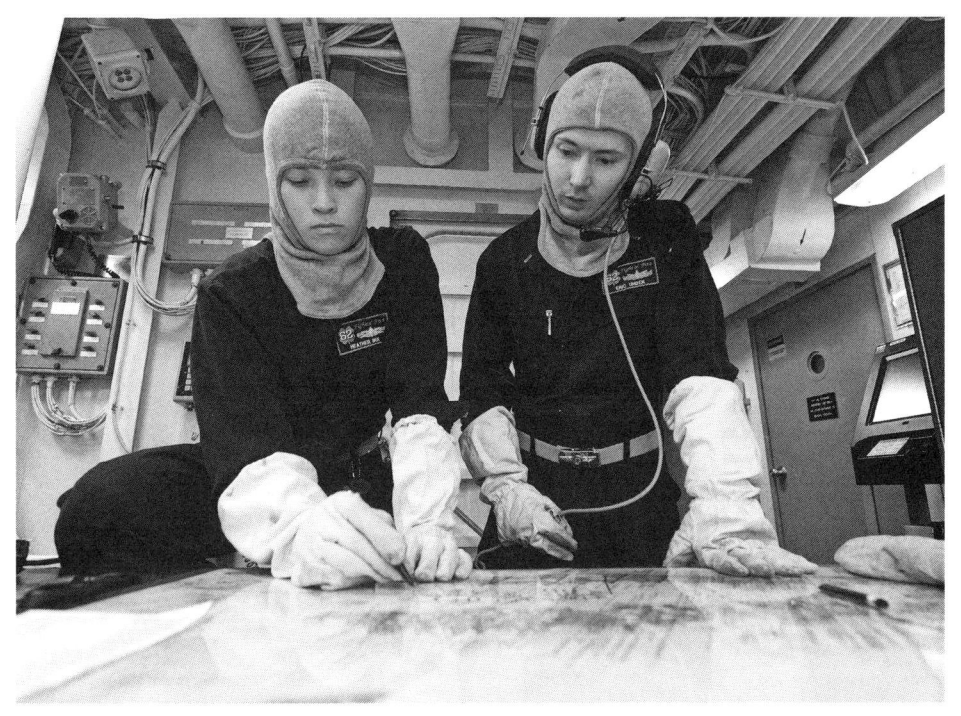

Leadership opportunities arise in many forms in the Navy. Here two ensigns serving as repair locker officers are plotting on a damage control chart.
U.S. Navy, MC2 William McCann

early and those briefing arriving much earlier than that. Simply put, making anyone—whether a seaman or an admiral—wait beyond the scheduled starting time of a meeting shows disrespect for his or her time.

You Are Part of a Watchstanding and Operational Culture

Whether you are working at a shore-based squadron (or office) that requires you to stand duty once a month or on a ship or submarine that requires you to stand watch several times a day, standing a good watch is one of the Navy's universal skill sets. No matter how quiet or mundane the duty, your leaders are counting on you to stand your watch or duty day professionally and with attention to detail. The notion of maintaining a presence in an otherwise empty building or command center outside normal working hours may seem strange, but some of the first measures of your professional performance will likely be qualifying to stand a basic watch or duty position.

More profound than the watchstanding culture itself will be your involvement in supporting military operations. Even if your job is to track parts or file reports in support of an operation, it is important to remember what the broader mission is: delivering persistent combat power to fight and win—or prevent—our nation's wars.

Support for Subordinates Is Defined Broadly

As a newly commissioned officer you will very likely be assigned a division officer role in providing "front-line" support for some of the Sailors under your command or in your workplace. Our greater society largely subscribes to the belief that only work-related conduct should be the concern of the employer when it comes to their employees' personal lives, but the Navy takes a much broader view.

This broader view is not surprising given that the nature of our work demands that Sailors be ready to deploy on a moment's notice with protracted periods of absence from their families. Sailors' finances, educational needs, and family living arrangements—issues that would be left to employees to figure out on their own in civilian organizations—will take up a surprising amount of your time. Like many things in life and in the Navy, an ounce of prevention often beats a pound of cure, and you will find that the very best leaders periodically check on their Sailors' needs rather than waiting for a crisis to occur.

You Will Be Running Things Sooner than You Think

In addition to serving their country, young officers most often cite early leadership opportunities as among the most satisfying aspects of their jobs. In very short order you will be running a watch team, leading a duty section, or overseeing an evolution at sea. Even if your first tasks are more administrative in nature, you will be expected to take the lead early, so be ready.

Read the Instructions

Whether you are preparing for a space inspection, conducting a flight deck emergency drill, or assisting in a burial at sea, there is a naval reference to guide you in your preparation for the event and, where appropriate, its grading criteria. Even when challenges emerge that are not as specific as a training exercise, you will often find—with a little effort—instructions, references, or lessons that can guide you in your preparation. One of the first questions you should ask yourself—and those who work for you—is "What is the reference?" because your seniors will surely be asking the same thing.

Leadership: A Universal Endeavor

Although each of you will face a wide variety of experiences dictated by service community and individual circumstances, your role as a leader binds you together with your peers and the generations of officers who have gone before you. Your command, your Sailors, and, most important, your nation deserve nothing less than your very best.

2

Your First Duty

Congratulations! You are a freshly commissioned officer in the U.S. Navy. College and your initial commissioning training are behind you, and you are ready for the adventure to begin. As with any new chapter in your life, you likely have more questions than answers. What happens now? What will be expected of you? How will you navigate the next few months as a newly commissioned officer—particularly if you are headed to an operational command right away? These are a few of the questions this chapter will help you answer.

You will find the next year to be challenging, to say the least. The period immediately ahead will be by turns exciting, interesting, difficult, and rewarding. You will discover more about your character and what you are capable of than many people will ever know in a lifetime. You are part of a long line of naval officers that stretches back to the dawn of the republic. Important work lies ahead!

Before You Report

The period before you actually check in to your new command will be a busy one. Packing, travel, and searching for a new place to live will absorb most of your time and attention. As you work through this period keep two things in mind:

- Communicate. Keep your new command fully informed of your plans, whereabouts, and any personal issues that come up. Ask questions.

Your First Duty ≈ 15

Even in your first job you will be making a difference. An ensign takes notes as he speaks with the master of a fishing boat during maritime security operations in the Persian Gulf.
U.S. Navy, MCC Daniel Sanford

- Get as much done as possible in your personal life *before* you report. Life on a warship—or even in a training command or office—is always busy (frequently bordering on hectic), and your first few weeks will be especially demanding. There may be little time for things like searching for an apartment or unpacking, particularly if you are heading to an operational command.

As the day when you must actually report to your command approaches, you may feel a bit apprehensive. This is normal. It may help to remember that tens of thousands of young officers have been through the exact same experience over the last two centuries, and most have weathered the experience just fine. Within a few short weeks you will be a fully acclimated member of your command.

Your Orders

As you neared commissioning, you received orders to your first command. You may or may not know exactly what job awaits you in your new ship or command, and you may or may not get some shore-based training en route. Your official Bureau of Naval Personnel (BUPERS) orders will tell you quite a bit, so take the time to read them carefully.

Part 1 of the standard official BUPERS orders will be addressed to your current command, your new ship, and any intermediate training commands you will attend on the way to the ship. Note that after the "BUPERS ORDER" line are listed the sequential order number, your name, your social security number, and your officer designator (in this example 1160 for a nonqualified surface warfare officer).

If there is a subsequent change issued to your orders (a not infrequent occurrence) a change number will appear after the BUPERS order number (e.g., "BUPERS Order: 0256 Change 1"). Note that under "Detaching Activity" and "Ultimate Activity" are two lines labeled EDD and EDA. These are your expected detachment date (EDD) from your current command and the expected date of your arrival (EDA) at your new command. Finally, note the last line under "Ultimate Activity": your "report no later than" date and time.

The First Page of Your Orders

Part 2 of your orders will provide a wealth of information in (relatively) plain language. Some of the things you will find here are specific directions to your detaching and ultimate commands to comply with various instructions such as security clearance requirements and medical screening. Further down, assorted paragraphs will help you on your way, listing such things as contact points for government housing at your new duty station and advice on shipping household goods. If you have any additional questions, be sure to ask your leaders at your commissioning detachment before you depart. Part 2 will also give specific instructions to the detaching command on travel if your ship is home-ported overseas or on deployment, which is discussed in depth in the "Getting to Your Command" section below.

Your Sponsor

When your new command receives a copy of your orders, a sponsor will be assigned to assist you with your transition and guide you through your first few

Figure 2-1
Sample Orders

```
R 251042Z JAN 18
FM COMNAVPERSCOM MILLINGTON TN//PERS412/PERS455//
TO NROTC BIGSTATE
USS FASTSHIP (DDG 200)
BT
UNCLAS //N01321//
MSGID/GENADMIN/COMNAVPERSCOM//
SUBJ/BUPERS ORDER//
RMKS/
BUPERS ORDER: 0256    123-45-6789/1115   (PERS-4128)
OFFICIAL CHANGE DUTY ORDERS FOR
ENS CHESTER NIMITZ,   USN
XXXXXXXXXXXXXXXXXXXXXXXXXXXXXXXXXXXXXXXXXXXXXXXXXXXXXXXXXXXXXXXX
IN CARRYING OUT/PROCESSING THESE ORDERS, BOTH PARTS ONE AND TWO
MUST BE READ AND LISTED INSTRUCTIONS COMPLIED WITH.
XXXXXXXXXXXXXXXXXXXXXXXXXXXXXXXXXXXXXXXXXXXXXXXXXXXXXXXXXXXXXXXX
P A R T     O N E
------- DETACHING ACTIVITY (M) -------
WHEN DIRECTED BY REPORTING SENIOR, DETACH IN SEP 18    EDD: SEP 18
FROM STU NROTC BIGSTATE                                UIC: 31405
PERMANENT DUTY STATION  CA, SAN DIEGO
FROM DUTY UNDER INSTRUCTION                            ACC: 342
PERSONNEL ACCOUNTING SUPPORT: PERSONNEL SUPPDET NAVPOSGRADS
UIC: 43073
------- ULTIMATE ACTIVITY (M) -------
REPORT NOT LATER THAN OCT 18                           EDA: OCT 18
TO USS FASTSHIP (DDG 200)                              UIC: 30465
PERMANENT DUTY STATION  VA, NORFOLK
FOR DUTY                                               ACC: 342
BSC: 99990
PRD: 0704
PERSONNEL ACCOUNTING SUPPORT: PERSUPPDET NORFOLK
UIC: 43099
- REPORT NOT LATER THAN 0700, 10 OCT 18.
------- ACCOUNTING DATA -------
MAC CIC: 3N3I65564177460
CIC: A83I62UM
PCS ACCOUNTING DATA:
N3I6 1761453.2251 T 188566 A8 3I6/2/U/M 3I6556417746
```

weeks. Within a week or so, you should receive e-mail from your sponsor with an introduction, contact data, and information on your new command and home port.

If you do not receive word within a few weeks, or if you simply cannot wait to get started, contact the ship to find out who your sponsor is. The best way to do this is to send an e-mail to your new XO or department head (you may have to make a creative guess at the e-mail address, but it will usually be similar to xo@ddg50.navy.mil or ops@cg47.navy.mil). Failing that, do an Internet search for the command's website or Facebook page and send an e-mail or message to the webmaster asking for the sponsor coordinator and your department head. One note: on smaller operational commands you can expect to see a more tailored outreach to you as a newly arriving crewmember; if you are heading to a shore command or training command, your contact with your new command may be a bit less personal.

Your sponsor's job is to answer questions, act as an intermediary between you and the ship's office (admin) on travel matters, and generally smooth your way. Not all sponsors are created equal—if you are not getting the information you need, then politely request the answers, but keep in mind that your sponsor is likely very busy with his or her own duties and responsibilities.

Writing a Letter to Your New Commanding Officer

"You never get a second chance to make a first impression" may be a cliché, but you should keep it in mind when you sit down to write a letter of introduction to your new commanding officer. It's not rocket science, but it does require some thought and attention to detail.

Your goal is to briefly introduce yourself, provide relevant contact information, fill the command in on any special personal issues that affect your immediate future, and give a sense of cheerful eagerness to get on with your new job. The letter will be read by your commanding officer (CO), executive officer (XO), and department head. Very likely, it will also make its way to your sponsor and the officer you will be relieving. Keep this larger audience in mind as you draft your letter; there are some infamous examples of poorly written (or tone deaf) letters of introduction floating around the fleet.

Below are a few tips on drafting your letter:

- Be brief and to the point without being cold. It is okay to let some of your personality shine through, but don't include frivolous personal details.
- Formal modes of address are appropriate. Find out the name of your new CO and begin with "Dear Captain XXX."
- Don't try to be funny—humor rarely translates well on paper, particularly in your first communication with your new CO.
- Include a full list of contact methods (addresses, phone numbers, and e-mail) and your travel plans between now and when you report on board.

- Give some brief personal details such as where you grew up, your commissioning source, and the names of your spouse and kids (if applicable).

The above list is not intended to intimidate you; it is presented merely so you can avoid some of the pitfalls that previous junior officers have fallen into. If you keep it positive and to the point and use the judgment that helped you earn your commission, your letter will serve you well.

Reporting to Your First Command

After receiving your orders and communicating with your new command, you will want to plan properly for the day you walk up to the quarterdeck of that command. While many new ensigns will be heading to training commands for their first assignment, reporting to an operational unit is often the most involved, so we will focus primarily on this challenge.

How Do I Get to My New Command?

When your orders are issued to an afloat command, your XO will work with the placement officer to send you to any schools that may be required for your specific job (termed "billet" in the Navy). In this case, the first leg of travel to intermediate schools is relatively straightforward. If you are traveling by commercial air, your sponsor will work with you and the ship's admin office to arrange an itinerary. Keep your sponsor informed! Before you leave, you will get an advance travel payment to see you through until you check in, whereupon you will file a travel claim to be reimbursed for additional expenses.

If your ship or submarine is at sea for a few days, you will usually check into the base Transient Personnel Unit (TPU) or into the squadron or strike group to which your command is attached. Once again, if you have questions regarding where to report, reach out to your sponsor for advice.

This process is relatively simple if your ship is based in the United States and is not currently deployed. For commands or detachments based overseas, you will need to complete a thorough suitability screening process for both you and any family members you are taking with you to your new home port. Contact your new ship early and often—your contacts will be well versed in this process if they are stationed overseas.

If your ship is deployed, you will need a "port call" message from the local transportation office. To arrange travel to the ship's port of call, you will want to know your ship's schedule. (Caution: A ship's movement information is usually classified data. You will likely not be able to talk about this openly on a commercial phone line or on the Internet.) Travel will be arranged in one of two ways. If you are near a major naval base, your ship's office can probably arrange travel directly. If you are located at a Naval Reserve Officers Training Corps (NROTC) unit far from a naval base, you will likely report to the TPU of the ship's squadron in the ship's home port to wait while travel is arranged.

Your First Day

Ensigns reporting to a ship or submarine will likely face a few more challenges than those reporting to a training command or office ashore. If this is the case with you, one of your first challenges will be to identify the pier where your ship or submarine is berthed, so be sure to e-mail or call ahead to your ship's sponsor to determine this information.

Once you have made your way to the ship's location, park near the command, taking care not to park in a reserved space. You will need to present your ID to the Sailors guarding the gate at the end of the pier. Next to the pier you will see your ship—a gray hull bristling with antennas, guns, and activity. Above you, at the top of the brow (gangplank), you will see the officer of the deck (OOD), usually in dress uniform. Take a deep breath and get ready to begin your first day.

Checking on Board

If you haven't visited a naval ship recently, figuring out how to cross the brow properly can be a bit intimidating. You may want to pause for a few moments and watch somebody else cross the brow so you can get the lay of the land. The sequence for reporting on board is as follows:

- Cross the brow to just before the gangway (the opening in the ship's rail). Face aft, come to attention, and salute the national ensign if you arrive on the ship between 0800 and sunset.
- Face the OOD, salute, and say, "Ensign Halsey, reporting as ordered."
- Show the OOD your ID card (tip: get it out of your wallet before you start up the brow) and step onto the quarterdeck.

The OOD will log your name in the deck log and call your sponsor. You should report in summer whites (short sleeves) in the summer or dress blues in the winter. Bring your orders, medical record, dental record, and all receipts that you received while moving from your commissioning source to your new command. Your command's admin office will use these receipts to start your travel claim and reimburse you for costs you incurred while moving.

What if your ship is in the shipyard? In this case, your ship may be deep inside a controlled industrial area (CIA) covered with hoses and electrical cables. The best thing to do is arrange for your sponsor to meet you at the shipyard gate with a hardhat and goggles. Failing that, report to the shipbuilding superintendent's (SHIPSUP) office and have someone there call the ship. Talk to your sponsor ahead of time about what uniform to report in—while in the shipyard you may need to report in the Navy working uniform (NWU) and steel-toed boots.

If you are not reporting to an afloat unit or an intense training course such as basic underwater demolition (BUD/S, for sea-air-land [SEAL] training), your first day at a training command (or an office) is likely to feel similar to your previous training and academic experiences. If you are reporting to a shore command, you will want to read your orders, use the contact information included therein, and make an effort to ensure that your command knows the day you are coming. A member of the admin team will likely endorse your orders after you present them, signaling that your leave or travel period is concluded, and you will begin the check-in process.

Almost all commands have a check-in process and a sponsor system, and your first few days will likely be dedicated to this endeavor. If you are first reporting to a training command, you can expect to be in-processed with your classmates en masse, so this check-in will likely resemble some of your precommissioning training check-ins. Regardless of the command to which you are reporting, try to make a dry run the day before you report so you do not add to the stress of your first day by getting lost or failing to find a parking spot.

The Rest of Your First Day

The rest of your day will be devoted to introductions, administrative matters at the ship's office, and probably a quick tour of the ship. This may feel a bit disorienting, but don't be discouraged; you will soon get the hang of things. You may meet your CO, XO, and department head, but formal check-in interviews will probably be scheduled for the following days.

If you have reported to a ship or to a command that is embarked on a ship, you will soon share a meal in the wardroom. Chapter 4 discusses etiquette in greater detail; be sure to review the procedures for dining with your sponsor before you report. If you are reporting to a squadron or a shore command, your lunch may be much more low-key, with your command sponsor perhaps taking you to lunch on or near the base.

If reporting to a ship, you will also be assigned a bunk and locker on your first day. If you are fortunate, it will be a bunk in one of the officers' staterooms, but you may be assigned to a bunk in overflow berthing—a section of enlisted berthing that is used if there is an excess of officers assigned to the ship. While this arrangement is not as comfortable as a stateroom, remember that it's temporary; you will be shifted to a stateroom as more senior division officers rotate off the ship.

The First Few Weeks

Your first weeks at your new command will be a whirlwind of strange acronyms, turning over (taking responsibility for) your new division, and standing your first watches. Keep your eyes and ears open and try to absorb as much as possible. The information below will give you a sense of what to expect.

Indoctrination, Personnel Qualifications Standards, and Warfare Qualification

Your first week at a command will very likely be devoted to the administrative requirements of checking in and a formal introduction class often known as "Indoc." On a ship, this orientation session will teach you such basics as afloat safety and the ship's organization and will touch on broader policy issues and regulations whether you are reporting afloat or ashore. One item you should ask for is the commanding officer's philosophy—it will likely be a one- or two-page memo that lays out his or her vision and expectations.

Very soon after checking in at an afloat command you will receive assignments related to the personnel qualification standards (PQS). PQS is the Navy's standardized system for qualification. It covers everything shipboard from how to conduct basic maintenance to the minimum knowledge standards required to qualify as the ship's tactical action officer (TAO). There are qualifications required for those serving ashore as well.

All PQS books (often referred to as cards) include a list of knowledge factors that must be mastered item by item. Most cards also include a variety of practical factors that involve actual physical demonstration of a skill by the trainee before it is "signed off." Watch station PQS such as OOD and engineering officer of the watch (EOOW) will also require you to stand watches under instruction. The final step for most PQS is a series of interviews, tests, and qualification boards (group interviews) designed to ensure your readiness to assume your new responsibilities.

If you are reporting to a ship or submarine, one of your most important tasks over the next year or so will be earning your surface warfare or submarine warfare pin, which signifies your full entry into the ranks of the seagoing profession. Achieving this milestone will take a great deal of your time and energy during your first sea tour. Along the way to earning your pin you will have to qualify for several watch positions, the most important of which is OOD.

Although many other tasks and priorities will be vying for your attention, give the warfare qualification process the attention it deserves—there is nothing more important professionally in your first tour than achieving surface warfare or submarine warfare qualification. Tactical competencies carry equal significance in other communities, although in some communities such as naval aviation and the special warfare communities you may have earned your warfare pin through an arduous training process prior to reporting to your first operational command.

Watchstanding

In many commands, and on every ship, standing watch lies at the very heart of our profession. Your competence as a watchstander will be one of the primary skills by which your contribution to your command will be judged. Take this task seriously—you literally have the lives of your shipmates in your hands.

Very soon after your arrival you will be assigned a watch station (on a surface ship you may stand watch as conning officer on your first day under way). You should devote yourself to doing this job right, but take heart—your fellow officers will not let you fail. For a great deal of outstanding advice on watchstanding, see the *Watch Officer's Guide,* 15th edition, by ADM James Stavridis and RADM Robert Girrier, available from the Naval Institute Press.

Your Division
Aside from qualification and watchstanding, your other great responsibility will be leading Sailors. If you are on a ship or submarine, you will be directly responsible for a division of Sailors and, very often, millions of dollars' worth of equipment. If you are reporting to a shore billet, you will likely be assigned some leadership responsibilities similar to the division officer's portfolio. Training, maintenance, administration, counseling, discipline, and ensuring the general welfare of your Sailors are just a few of the tasks you will face.

Once again, take the job seriously, but do not allow yourself to become too anxious about how you will perform. Your CPO and more seasoned officers will spend a great deal of time teaching you the fundamentals of leadership and divisional management. For much more on the art and science of divisional leadership, see the superb *Division Officer's Guide,* which opens with a quote from one of our greatest naval leaders, ADM Arleigh Burke: "The division officer is the core of the Navy's spirit."

Your Boss
In a typical afloat billet your immediate superior will be one of the department heads (on most ships the weapons officer, combat systems officer, operations officer, chief engineer, or supply officer). Each department head is responsible for up to one-quarter of the ship's crew and equipment and has many collateral duties, including the training of junior officers and standing the most difficult watches on the ship. In other words, your department heads will be very busy.

Regardless of where your first command is located, you will almost certainly be reporting to a department or branch head, a senior officer placed above you in a chain of command that leads to the commanding officer and the executive officer. As a division officer you will work closely with your department head on the day-to-day operation of your command and planning for the future. A professional department head will do everything possible to train and mentor you but will expect *you* to *lead* your division, look into the future, plan, carry out the policies of the commanding officer, and most of all, *keep him or her informed*.

Basic Shipboard Organization

Not every ensign will be stationed on a ship; nevertheless, you will see elements of basic shipboard organization in most commands you might join as a newly commissioned officer. Most ensigns reporting to an afloat unit will serve as a division officer in charge of a group responsible for a specific set of equipment or tasks. Your division functions as part of a department with a broad portfolio of tasks vital to the ship's overall mission (e.g., engineering, combat systems, operations, supply). Your department head in turn reports to the XO, the second most senior officer on the ship, who is directly responsible to the CO for the overall operation of the ship.

The term "chain of command" describes the interrelationships between the various levels of authority on a given ship, squadron, or shore command. This chain starts with the lowest-ranking seaman or fireman, working up through work center supervisor, LPO, leading chief petty officer (LCPO), division officer, department head, to the executive officer and commanding officer. The chain of command is in effect the organization's nervous system: direction flows down the chain while information flows up.

Each level in the chain of command is expected to execute the mission within its span of control and to handle problems at the lowest level possible while keeping higher levels informed. This last element is especially important: "Keep the chain of command informed" is a mantra you will hear throughout your naval career (another popular saying is "Don't be the senior person with a secret"). You will often hear leaders exhorting Sailors to use the chain of command—and this is sound advice. Keep in mind that the ship's organization is not intended to be a "stovepipe" through which information is rigidly controlled. You will be expected to work closely with your peers in other divisions to solve problems and efficiently execute the command's mission.

If you are serving at sea on a surface ship, you will likely be initially assigned a watch station such as conning officer, reporting to the OOD. This will quickly be followed by underway watch assignments leading to more advanced watches and qualifications such as combat information center watch officer (CICWO), OOD, and EOOW. Typically, you will stand one or two three-to-five-hour watches in a day at sea, although this varies greatly with the pace of current operations and the number of persons qualified to fill out the watchbill.

In port, ensigns in afloat assignments will often be assigned as in-port OOD before moving on to standing one of the duty department head positions, responsible for your department in the absence of your department head (e.g., duty operations officer or engineering duty officer [EDO]). You will report to the command duty officer (CDO), a seasoned officer responsible for the daily conduct of the ship's routine while in port.

You will also be assigned to a duty section soon after you check in. Duty sections have responsibility for the ship for a twenty-four-hour period while in port, during which you will likely be assigned one or two watches. The remainder of the day you will be on board to supervise your department's duty section, act as a "damage control" reserve in the case of emergency, and defend the ship against outside attack. Most ships rotate through six duty sections while in their home port and through three sections while deployed overseas.

If you are reporting to a training or shore command, your watchstanding and duty responsibilities may vary. Regardless of which watch or duty section you are assigned, you will want to approach the job seriously, work hard to get qualified so that you can return value to the organization, and, once qualified, aim to be ready to learn and fill the next senior position.

Some Basics on Shipboard Life and Naval Protocol

The U.S. Navy is an organization that prides itself on honoring tradition. Shipboard protocol is based on traditional military values and rituals that extend back to the birth of the U.S. Navy and even further back to the Royal Navy; it exists as a common framework across the many generations of our Navy.

As in all military organizations, there exists a fine balance between deference to senior rank and the close bond between shipmates built up over months of close and difficult service together. That balance is always in play, and it is sometimes difficult for a new officer to discern the line between proper deference and the unique camaraderie of a military unit. This section is intended to help you navigate your first few months on board. Below are some tips to orient you in the right direction.

Junior-Senior Officer Relationships

In theory, every officer on board has a distinct seniority based on rank and date of commissioning (a lineal number). In practice, most wardrooms or aviation squadrons are composed of three groups: the CO and XO, the department heads, and the division officers (often referred to as the JOs, although technically any officer below the rank of commander is a junior officer). Relations between division officers will tend toward the informal use of first names (in private), while your relationship with department heads and above will be much more formal.

A nuance in this system is positional authority; sometimes an officer of junior rank is assigned to a job that entails supervision of officers technically senior, most commonly when a department head is junior to one of his or her division officers. In this case, precedence goes to whoever is senior by *position*, not rank (although sensible officers will certainly take actual rank into account when dealing with each other). When in doubt, tend to formality toward your seniors.

Relations with Enlisted Sailors

In the vast majority of naval communities, your default position should be toward formality without being stuffy. Over time you will develop a certain amount of comfort with the people who work for you. This is neither unexpected nor discouraged (after all, most of your Sailors are hard-working, smart, dedicated professionals, just like you). However, you must be careful to draw the line appropriately—occasional good humor or conversations about family are fine, but you must discourage undue familiarity that tends toward a first-name relationship. In all cases, you *must* avoid favoritism or fraternization, whether real or perceived.

Relations with Your Chief

How can you be expected to supervise a man or woman who is considerably older than you are and has much more experience? This may be one of the thorniest issues you will encounter on your first tour. The quality of CPOs can vary widely: at one end of the spectrum is the chief who can do her or his job (and yours) with ease; at the other extreme—and much rarer—there will be

CPOs who will need some prodding to fulfill their duties (to be fair, you will find the same phenomenon in the officer corps). Fortunately for the U.S. Navy, the vast majority of CPOs are highly competent and understand their role not only as divisional leaders but also as mentors of their division officers.

A sound approach to take toward your chief is an adaptation of President Ronald Reagan's saying, "Trust but verify." In other words, defer to your chief's skill and experience, but seek out the underlying facts for your own evaluation. "Chief, can you please show me the reference" is never a bad request, least of all for your own education.

Formality on Watch

There is no room for compromise regarding formality on watch. Sadly, this is a lesson that has been written in blood; informal communications have been the cause of many a tragedy at sea. Formal repeat back of orders, focus on the task at hand, a questioning attitude, and strict adherence to established procedures are crucial at all times when on watch.

After-Hours Protocol

Your entire wardroom will socialize together periodically, and you will almost certainly spend some time hanging out with your peers. You will develop close friendships with some of your fellow JOs and to some extent even with more senior officers. While a greater degree of informality will be expected in a social setting, the same basic shipboard rules on deference apply.

You will also on occasion interact with enlisted Sailors in a more social setting, either at command-sponsored functions or occasional divisional events. By all means, spend some time in conversation with your folks at the command picnic or make a brief appearance at a divisional party, but be careful not to cross the line into fraternization and undue familiarity. Think of it as a sort of "one drink" rule of thumb: spend enough time with your Sailors to converse over one beer or soda, then politely move on.

Social Media Conduct

Social media is a great way to reach out to your command prior to reporting and also to network and socialize with fellow Navy members throughout the course of your career. Although there are many benefits to social media, you should be cautious in your conduct on social media platforms and always be aware that you are a representative of the U.S. Navy. ADM John M. Richardson, 31st Chief of Naval Operations (CNO), highlights the following guidance for social media conduct:

- Consider what messages are being communicated and how they could be received.
- Create or share content that is consistent with Navy values.
- Only post or share messages or content that demonstrate dignity and respect for yourself and others.

Many of your Sailors at your new command will reach out to you on social media to "follow" or "friend" you. Allowing this connection is permitted and at your discretion; however, you should follow the aforementioned guidance on interactions with Sailors and conduct yourself in a virtual environment the same way you would at your command. In some cases, having social media connections with your Sailors can be beneficial, such as getting in touch with them when on liberty during deployment or if they are having communication issues and have no other means of contact.

Common sense is a good guide to shipboard and online protocol and general etiquette. These topics are discussed in greater detail later in this book.

Uniform Matters

The Uniform Regulations cover uniform matters in exhaustive detail. Every officer is expected to maintain a complete seabag of uniforms, and the importance of setting an example for your Sailors in terms of both having the right uniform and wearing it well cannot be overemphasized. This section gives a brief primer on uniforms for seagoing officers.

What Do Seagoing Officers Really Wear?

What you wear under way will vary among commands. On ships and submarines, the two basic schemes are either NWUs or coveralls, each with steel-toed boots and an eight-point cover or command ball cap. All ships require fire-retardant coveralls in all spaces, which you will be issued upon arrival. You will also be issued a foul-weather jacket for use on watch (this jacket is customarily not worn off ship).

When in port, you will routinely wear NWUs, but you should always have a set of poly-wool khakis in hot standby on the ship—there will be many occasions when you will be required to greet a dignitary visiting the ship, visit a higher headquarters, or have a meeting off ship with little or no notice. Aviators will most often wear a flight suit in the work environment, but check with your more senior JOs to determine when a more formal uniform is required: for example, when visiting various parts of a base or dining in a more formal section of the wardroom on a ship. Finally, if you are a newly commissioned ensign serving at a shore command, you will likely be wearing poly-wool khakis or type I or III NWUs, but uniforms will vary if you are attending an operational school.

What Else Should I Take with Me?

If you are reporting to your ship before deployment, you will have plenty of opportunity to figure out what to take with you. Be sure to confer with your ship's sponsor, since he or she will have specific insight into what is normally worn and needed on the ship or command to which you are reporting. The basics include uniforms for in port and under way, the seasonal dress uniform, toiletries, physical training (PT) gear, professional reading material, and clothes for liberty (bringing business attire such as a jacket and tie for men and the equivalent for women is recommended).

Conclusion

As you prepare for one of the greatest transitions in your life, you will no doubt have many more questions than were answered here. Nevertheless, this chapter will get you headed in the right direction. Rest assured that within a few short weeks you will be a fully integrated member of your command, and within a year you will be a seasoned officer others will turn to for answers.

3

Naval Customs

Many organizations have their unique set of customs, but very few organizations equal the U.S. Navy in the strength that our service draws from our traditions. As a newly commissioned ensign you will likely encounter a greater variety of customs and courtesies in the Navy than you did in previous chapters of your life. The good news is that the basics of naval courtesy and customs are not only relatively simple but have also been covered in commissioning pipelines such as the U.S. Naval Academy, Naval Reserve Officers Training Corps (NROTC), and officer indoctrination courses for those earning a commission from the fleet.

There are a number of books that describe our service's customs exceptionally well. *Naval Courtesies, Customs, and Traditions* would be a fine addition to any naval officer's professional library; it covers both the history of the customs and their current use. For a shorter but very practical overview of naval customs, refer to *The Bluejacket's Manual,* the definitive guide for Sailors of all ranks. The *Manual* contains a superb chapter titled "Navy Customs, Courtesies, and Ceremonies" that addresses the basics extremely well.

What Is So Special about Navy Customs?

If you have not spent much time in the Navy or as a member of a naval family, you may be wondering why these customs and conventions are so important and why people in the Navy spend so much time focusing on their appropriate observances and execution. Thomas J. Cutler, author of *The Bluejacket's Manual*, once wrote, "Once you have been to sea, or flown on a naval air mission, or taken part in the many different things that Sailors the world over are doing every hour of every day, you will know from firsthand experience how different a job in the Navy can be from what your counterparts in civilian life are doing. It is only fitting, therefore, that we celebrate our uniqueness through special ceremonies and demonstrate our differences through special customs that remind us of our very different heritage."

Navy customs are in most cases fairly simple, and they not only celebrate our heritage but also give Sailors the opportunity to hone their attention to detail. As you progress in your naval career, you will often find that commands that do the "little" things well—salutes, rendering honors, and standing a taut quarterdeck watch—are equally adept at the more complex, mission-oriented competencies. This is not a coincidence, and you will find that adherence to naval customs both reminds us of our heritage and provides an opportunity to correctly practice the little things that can make a big difference.

Saluting

Saluting is one of the basic expressions of respect that a junior shows to a senior officer. Very simply, you give a hand salute by raising your right hand sharply until your fingertips touch the edge of your cover just to the right of your right eye. Your upper arm should be parallel to the ground, and your fingers should form a straight line to your elbow. Your thumb and fingers should be extended and together with your palm down. You conclude the salute by returning your hand fluidly down to your side.

Naval personnel render salutes only in uniform, when covered. If you are walking toward a senior officer, you give a salute ten to fifteen feet before you reach the officer and hold your salute until the senior returns it. As you salute, you are expected to give a short greeting ("Good morning, sir [or ma'am]" before noon; "Good afternoon, sir [or ma'am]" between 1200 and 1800; or "Good evening, sir [or ma'am]" after 1800). In addition to returning your salute, the senior officer will customarily return your greeting. When you are saluted, you should always return the greeting as well as the salute.

Saluting on Board a Ship

Saluting on a ship incorporates a few additional customs. First, when you board a ship that is flying the national ensign, stop a few feet before you actually step on the ship, turn to and salute the flag (usually aft on the stern), and then pivot to salute the officer of the deck. When you leave the ship, give your salutes in reverse order—the OOD first, then the national ensign.

On a ship, if you are covered (usually outside or on the bridge), you will salute a flag officer, the CO, and visiting officers senior to the CO each time you encounter them. For other officers who are senior to you, render a salute during your first meeting with them during the day.

Greetings

Whether you are outdoors or indoors ashore (or inside a ship at sea), greetings are a very important part of the Navy's social and military fabric. Even in close quarters and after repeated encounters during the day, it is always acceptable and appropriate to look someone in the eye and greet them appropriately—regardless of whether they are senior or junior. Always greet a senior officer, and never fail to respond positively to someone who has greeted you.

The Quarterdeck

Ships, and many shore commands, have a quarterdeck where watchstanders officially greet guests and control access to the broader command area. These areas almost always feature the national ensign and the Navy flag and should be traversed with respect. If you are entering the quarterdeck to visit the command, follow the directions of the officer or petty officer in charge—he or she is a direct representative of the commanding officer.

The general custom is that you should avoid crossing the quarterdeck unless it is absolutely necessary. If you must do so, it is customary to ask permission of the OOD before crossing. Customs vary more broadly ashore, so be sure to ask another junior officer what is expected at your command.

National Anthem and Colors

While most of us have some familiarity with the basic customs related to the national anthem, this is a custom that those who wear "the cloth of our nation" must get right. When the national anthem is played and you are covered, face the national ensign if it is displayed, salute on the anthem's first note, and conclude your salute on the last note. If the flag is not displayed, face in the direction of the music instead. If you are in civilian clothes, stand at attention, place your right hand over your heart (rather than saluting), and follow the same facing directions as for those in uniform. If you are wearing a ball cap or hat in civilian clothes, follow the same steps but place the hat over your heart with your right hand.

On military installations, you will also encounter saluting requirements during morning and evening colors. Morning colors occurs at 0800 and is preceded by a short preparatory signal at 0755; it commences with the national anthem being played as the national ensign is raised. If you are outside, you are expected to face the national ensign and hold your salute during the national anthem. At sunset, evening colors is also preceded by a preparatory signal five minutes before "Taps" is played as the national ensign is lowered. Once again, you maintain your salute during the playing of "Taps." If you are on base and in a car, you are expected to bring the car to rest until colors is completed, if it is safe to do so.

Wardroom Etiquette

Wardrooms are the living room, dining room, and boardroom for most at-sea commands. These spaces often contain some of the ship's most valued possessions and are decorated more nicely than other working spaces on the ship. Not surprisingly, eating in the wardroom requires a little more thought than eating at an informal meal with your family or in a college cafeteria, but after a few meals the habits will come naturally:

- Before you enter, leave your ball cap/cover outside the wardroom.
- If a senior officer is already seated, request permission to join the mess.
- Be on time for meals. At lunch and dinner, you will stand at your seat until the senior officer (usually the CO on small ships) invites everyone to sit down.
- If you are late, request permission to join the mess late, but avoid making lateness a habit.
- Avoid talking only about work and stick to topics of conversation that are appropriate for everyone at the table.

- Treat every guest well. If you are seated near another shipmate's guest, be pleasant and attempt to include that person in your conversation. If you bring a guest, be sure to introduce that person to the wardroom.
- If you must leave the meal early, ask the senior person at the table to be excused.

Wardroom customs vary from ship to ship. Meals are reminiscent of a happy family dinner in some wardrooms, while other wardrooms are more formal. On some ships, coveralls and flight suits are acceptable; other wardrooms require officers to change into a more formal uniform. In some commands, holding meetings and doing individual work in the wardrooms are necessities, whereas other ships strictly reserve the use of the wardroom for meals and a brief stop for coffee. Your best advice for navigating wardroom customs will come from your shipmates who have preceded you. You in turn should help the next ensign who follows your arrival—they will have many of the same questions you do.

Interacting with Seniors

In a time and culture in which employees frequently refer to their bosses by first name, the military stands apart in the respect that our service accords to senior leaders. In addition to rendering a salute to a senior officer, there are several other courtesies you should follow.

- If you are seated, stand up when a senior leader enters a room or space.
- When you walk with the senior, stay to his or her left.
- When entering a small boat such as a barge or a liberty boat, enter first and leave last.
- In automobiles, the senior should be offered the most desirable seat. Traditionally, in a passenger car with a driver this is the right window seat in the backseat, but in vans or personal cars the senior may wish to take the front seat.
- Always offer a seat to a senior.
- Never make a senior officer wait.
- Don't make excuses. When interacting with a senior in a professional setting, the five basic responses ("yes, sir"; "no, sir"; "aye, aye, sir"; "I'll find out, sir"; and "no excuse, sir") are superb guides to follow.

Ceremonies and Events You May Encounter

The variety and conduct of U.S. Navy ceremonies are too extensive to list in this small chapter, but there are a few core ceremonies that you can expect to see in your first year or two of service.

Change of Command

The high mobility of our profession virtually ensures that you will participate in a change of command as a junior officer. Command is the most cherished leadership role that exists in the U.S. Navy, so it is not surprising that we pause to formally recognize the turnover of command from one leader to another. The uniform for these events can range from service dress whites (choker whites) to wash khakis if the change of command is held at sea.

Because a change-of-command ceremony will often require effort in advance of the actual day's events, you may be tasked to provide support for the event. As a junior officer, you may serve as an usher, a quarterdeck watchstander, or even a supervisor of a VIP parking area during the event. Your chief and you will also be expected to ensure that you and your Sailors are in the right uniform. Regardless of your duties, give this ceremony the attention and respect it deserves.

Burial at Sea

If you are serving in an afloat command, your ship may play a role in providing those who have served their final resting place. These events strictly follow the fleet guidance, including providing the families with a videotape and letter describing their loved one's ceremony. Junior officers are often asked to stand in ranks or assist in the disposition of the deceased's ashes.

Ship Christenings and Commissionings

Bringing a ship to life from construction is one of the most challenging and memorable opportunities naval officers experience in their professional life. Chapter 2 of *Command at Sea* contains a superb synopsis of this process, which usually includes a christening ceremony and culminates with a commissioning ceremony. The ship's christening occurs in the yard where the ship is being built and largely focuses on the namesake of the ship and the workers who are building it. If you are attached to the ship at the time of the christening, you will be expected to attend and will likely march with the other members of your command. The high point of this event occurs when the ship's sponsor breaks a bottle of champagne across the bow of the new ship.

The ship's commissioning, which marks the ship's formal entry into the fleet, usually takes place in a port other than the shipyard and occurs on a Friday or Saturday after a week's worth of activities in the commissioning port. This ceremony is almost always a formal event with participants in service dress whites or service dress blues with medals and swords. As a junior officer, you will likely participate in several extensive rehearsals to make sure that the ceremony—often attended by thousands—and the cocktail parties held to celebrate the occasion go well. Once again it is essential to make sure that you and your Sailors have the right uniforms and understand your roles in each event.

Reenlistments and Retirements

You will likely have a Sailor reenlist during your first year. Reenlistment is an important milestone because the Sailor commits an additional part of his or

Honors and ceremonies, such as this christening ceremony, are an integral part of the U.S. Navy's heritage.
Courtesy Bath Iron Works

her life to the Navy. In most commands, reenlistment will involve a small ceremony, the oath of enlistment, and presentation of a few reenlistment benefits, all of which the Sailor's family members are likely to attend. If you are a division officer, you will not want to take these events lightly; make sure that they are well attended by your other Sailors and supported by the command. If your Sailor selects you as the reenlisting officer, view this as the honor it is and make sure you are prepared to administer the oath, ideally from memory to demonstrate the care and interest this event deserves.

You will occasionally encounter members of your command who are concluding their careers. Retirement ceremonies are deeply valued in the Navy culture because they are our last opportunity to acknowledge that person's service. If you are asked to support this event, do so to the best of your ability because the retiring member has literally given the very best years of his or her adult life to the Navy.

Crossing the Line

Although this ceremony has evolved over the years, crossing the equator is a significant milestone in a Sailor's life. During this event, "shellbacks"—those who have crossed the equator before—oversee the induction of "polliwogs" into this sacred brotherhood. The ceremony concludes with the polliwogs being cleansed with saltwater and deemed worthy by King Neptune and Davy Jones (the most senior shellbacks).

If you are crossing the line for the first time, your responsibilities will be limited to participating in the event and keeping your sense of humor. Although the vast majority of these ceremonies are properly and safely executed, over the years a very few have descended into hazing or inappropriate treatment of some crewmembers. Rest assured that the senior members of your chain of command will be watching carefully to prevent that from occurring.

Dining In and Dining Out

In the Navy, a "dining in" traditionally refers to a wardroom-only event held on the ship or in a private dining area. Traditionally, officers wear mess dress (or another formal uniform), and "the Vice," usually a seasoned member of the wardroom, serves as the host and closely monitors the behavior of all participants during the toasts, the meal, and the speaker's remarks.

As the ceremony nears completion, the Vice will assess "charges" to those members who have committed an etiquette or uniform infraction, with punishments varying from drinking "grog" to singing a song or telling a joke. Once the dinner begins, guests are not permitted to leave—even to go to the restroom—so be sure to watch your liquid intake. In some commands, dining ins now include the chiefs' mess.

"Dining outs" traditionally include the spouses or dates of the wardroom and almost always occur off ship in a private dining room. Like the dining in, there is a Vice who monitors and enforces good behavior and decorum, so be sure to share these customs with your spouse or date because you may be held "accountable" for his or her infractions! Once again, these events are generally conducted with a spirit of fun, so enjoy yourself. While the associated customs may seem old-fashioned or too much of an effort to prepare for, they are often some of the most memorable events of a tour, and they bind us to the generations of officers before us who participated in similar events.

Official Calls

Older books on military etiquette give considerable space to the mechanics of how an officer "makes a call" on a senior officer, usually his or her CO. Fortunately, in today's Navy this custom has been replaced by two relatively simple events. First, you will almost always meet with your CO within the first week or so of arriving at your new command. In small at-sea commands, this may be the first of many encounters with your CO. In larger commands, it may be some time before you meet the captain again. In either case, you will want to be prepared to talk about your background and goals for your time as a member of the captain's team. Additionally, you will want to make sure that you are in a good uniform, well groomed, and ready to engage the CO positively—first impressions can last a long time.

The second component of this process is usually a "Hail and Farewell," covered more extensively in chapter 4 of this book. This social gathering, often hosted at an officer's home, collectively serves to welcome those who have newly arrived and bid farewell to those leaving the command. Generally, Hail and Farewells occur every two to three months and can be among the social rituals that you will remember fondly as you grow older.

While the custom of "calling" on senior officers has evolved significantly, if you are on an afloat command, this custom still survives when your CO is visiting other ports. As a junior officer on duty, you may be detailed to escort or drive your CO on such visits, which usually last fifteen to thirty minutes, often involve coffee or tea, and conclude with an exchange of small gifts. If you are directed to assist, make sure that you are in the right uniform, are well groomed, and are paying attention—in a few short years, you may be a young CO doing the same thing.

Foreign Customs

Although it might seem hard to believe after reviewing the number of ceremonies in this chapter, our military customs reflect the informality of American culture. Military customs in many other cultures tend to be much more formal. If you anticipate having to play a role in ceremonies or calls involving international services or international locations, a thorough review of that nation's customs and history is warranted.

On a ship, you will be able draw upon the experience of those who have served overseas; they will ensure that you attend the "port brief" that customarily occurs after a ship pulls into a foreign port. Through e-mail at sea, your command will also be able to reach out to protocol experts off the ship to make sure that you are abiding by the customs that will represent you and the U.S. Navy most appropriately to your hosts.

Conclusion

Naval customs provide a common framework for naval personnel to interact and work well together. More important, these customs also embody the tradition and core values that are integral to our service's heritage. While these customs may warrant additional review and effort, cherish them—they help to create the foundation of our naval service, binding together naval generations past, present, and future.

4

Social Etiquette

Dr. Robert Fulghum wrote a popular book in the 1980s, *All I Really Need to Know I Learned in Kindergarten*, which emphasized that we learn most of the basics of human interaction as young children—and this certainly applies to social etiquette. Although the word "etiquette" may evoke stiff, formal dinners or the rules that prepare one to participate in such an event, the reality is that etiquette provides a framework of consideration, respect, and consistency for our social interactions. Some rules of etiquette may seem old-fashioned, but you will always be well served if you approach social dealings with the intent to be respectful of others' feelings.

The principal reference on etiquette for the naval officer is *Service Etiquette* (5th edition) by Cherlynn Conetsco and Anna Hart and is available at most U.S. Navy uniform shops on base. Although the rise of e-mail and a general loosening of formality have changed the social landscape since *Service Etiquette* was last updated, it remains a valuable and comprehensive reference. This chapter is not a substitute for a comprehensive guide on etiquette, but it does provide an overview of the basics that pertain to the majority of social issues you will encounter as a newly commissioned naval officer.

If it has been a while since you have reviewed social customs for writing thank-you notes and tipping a waiter or baggage handler, consider investing in a basic etiquette book. Your social life at college or your prior enlisted experience likely comprised informal get-togethers and social events, but you will encounter a broader range of social activities as a naval officer. Of the many etiquette books available, one of the better known and accepted versions is *Emily Post's Etiquette* by Lizzie Post and Daniel Senning. Regardless of which book you choose, most of them cover similar ground, and most advice aligns fairly closely from book to book. Be sure to pick a book that you find readable and user-friendly—a book that is too large or intimidating for everyday use will never help you if it merely sits on your shelf.

General Socializing and Entertaining

One aspect of naval life that officers usually remember long after their service is the socializing they enjoyed with friends in the Navy. Although socializing in the Navy is not as formal as World War II–era movies depict or as raucous as movies such as *Top Gun* portray, it will likely be more structured than what you experienced in college or in your previous service as an enlisted Sailor.

In many ways, the social transition you make from your previous life to your social life as an officer will be very similar to what a young professional experiences after leaving college for his or her first workplace. There will still be time for you to socialize with your closest friends in an environment and style comfortable for you, but you will also find that your social group will very naturally expand to include the people you work with. Socializing with coworkers is common in most professions, and many who share your profession will share other interests as well.

Yet because you will live, travel, and operate with your coworkers, socializing in a Navy command—particularly a deployable command—often takes on greater significance for officers and their families. While some "career strategists" may assert that socializing within in the wardroom is critical to your success and must be carefully managed, this is more urban legend than fact. Certainly some social commitments will come with being a part of a naval command, but in many ways they will be no more demanding than what would be expected of a member of a civilian executive team in which meeting with clients and coworkers is an expected part of the job.

More important than any perceived professional benefit is having friends with whom to share the Navy experience. With this in mind, investing in your naval experience by participating in social events—whether they include grabbing an informal meal or participating in an organized event such as a command dining out—will make your new, broader life even richer.

Some general advice: be yourself and do what you enjoy. As an officer candidate or midshipman you had many social experiences that will be similar to those you will encounter in the Navy. And look forward to the new experiences.

Meals

Reviewing general table manners will be a worthwhile endeavor if you have eaten most of your recent meals in a college cafeteria or other informal eating environment. Rest assured that most of the people you will be dining with were not raised in a country club or formal environment either, so reviewing table manners before a formal meal is something that many of us have to do.

Whether you review *Service Etiquette* or a more general etiquette book, the basics remain the same. As you face your plate, remember the acronym "BMW," like the car, which corresponds to "bread, meal, water." This will remind you that you will use the bread plate on the left side of your dinner plate and drink

Not all social events in the military are formal. Here a wardroom enjoys a wetting-down ceremony celebrating an officer's promotion.
Courtesy USS Stockdale *(DDG 106)*

from the glass (or glasses) on your right. Place your napkin in your lap; never tuck it into your collar or belt. When you leave the table, place the napkin, loosely folded, to the left of your plate. It is customary to pass things in a counterclockwise direction. Avoid reaching for things; instead ask someone closer to it to pass the item to you. Just as your parents may have reminded you as a child, sitting up straight, chewing with your mouth closed, and not speaking with your mouth full are basic rules to follow.

Hosting or Organizing an Event

At some point early in your career you may want to host your own social event and include some of your wardroom counterparts when you invite a few friends over to watch a football game or a movie. Your event will not be expected to equal one a senior officer hosts, but a few guidelines will assist you in making the event a success.

Keep It Simple

If you are hosting an actual command or departmental event, keeping things simple is fine. Many naval events, even full wardroom social functions, are potluck, so your guests will not find it odd if your invitation requests that they bring a side dish or another item if they choose to participate. You are certainly not required to provide alcohol at an event you host, but if you do, make sure to have nonalcoholic beverages as well.

Be Inclusive

If you are hosting a party or an event that can easily include more participants (as opposed to a dinner where space will limit whom you can include), try to bring in members of the wardroom in a way that does not make anyone feel excluded. Although being inclusive is important, you are certainly allowed to socialize with just one or two friends or couples from the ship as well. Going to dinner or participating in a common interest often naturally limits the size of a group for a given event. As with any other group of people, you will be drawn to some peers more naturally than others, but avoid setting a social pattern that could be perceived as a clique. There are few things more divisive in an otherwise good wardroom than the development of cliques among officers—or their spouses.

Consider Activities beyond Your Home

If the size of your home does not allow you to entertain in large numbers, consider organizing an outing somewhere else. Shared interests in sports, music, movies, or even a certain type of food (barbecue, ethnic food, etc.) provide the common ground that has initiated many lifelong friendships. The Navy's morale, welfare, and recreation (MWR) program provides opportunities to try new activities that may become lifelong hobbies. Many officers have developed a love of fishing, golf, tennis, or sailing after trying these activities for the first time as junior officers. While you should not feel compelled to pick up an activity merely because your boss enjoys it, if you are genuinely interested in an activity and have been invited to participate, give it a try.

Fun Things to Do

In addition to organizing social events for your own enjoyment, you may be asked to come up with an activity for your wardroom, office, or department. Here are a few activities to consider. Many of these may be supported or discounted by the MWR center on your nearest naval installation:

- Attending regional festivals
- Eating out as group at a gourmet or ethnic restaurant
- Hosting a football party
- Spending a day at the beach for a volleyball party
- Running a 5K or 10K as a wardroom or command
- Visiting a museum or an art exhibit
- Visiting national and state parks or historic sites together
- Attending a concert or play
- Attending major or minor league baseball games or other athletic events
- Visiting a comedy club
- Going deep sea fishing
- Performing a community service project as a group

Not every one of these events will be a good fit for every group—particularly a larger, "all-wardroom" event—but most people enjoy and appreciate events that offer variety and a departure from the norm.

Responding to Invitations

During your first tour as an ensign you will almost certainly receive an invitation to a social event hosted by another officer, often someone senior to you. Remember to respond in a timely and appropriate manner. Usually an invitation will indicate if the host expects you to reply and will provide an e-mail, phone number, or response card to do so. If a response is requested, respond with a "yes" or "no" via the manner described on the invitation (unless the invitation indicates regrets only).

Remembering that most etiquette is based on consideration, respect, and consistency, it should be obvious why responding promptly is so important. On a practical level, your host will want to have a good idea of how many people will be coming in order to appropriately prepare. Additionally, there is nothing more dispiriting for hosts than being left to wonder how many guests will come to an event for which they have made extensive preparations. Remember the Golden Rule and think about how you would want to be treated if you were hosting an event.

If you do accept an invitation, it is always nice to offer to bring something to support the host's effort. If, after inquiring what you can bring, the host replies that he or she does not need any assistance, a small token of thanks such as a bottle of wine or flowers will always be appreciated. Once you have accepted an invitation, make every effort to attend. This is the considerate thing to do, and it points to your general efforts to keep your promises and commitments.

Social and Personal Conduct as an Officer

As a commissioned officer you represent the Navy twenty-four hours a day, seven days a week. This may sound overly dramatic or even burdensome, but it is unfailingly true. Even if you are on leave or off duty, your good personal conduct or your failure to meet Navy standards will reflect on your command, your shipmates, and our service. Simply put, you will want your conduct to be such that your parents—or the parents of your Sailors—would be proud.

Although the vast majority of young officers conduct themselves admirably, even the most upright people sometimes lose their way. Most shortfalls in conduct stem from a lack of judgment rather than a lack of character, and nothing accelerates this process more than the abuse of alcohol. Remember that how you dress, the events you attend, what you post online, and even the businesses you patronize can also reflect on the Navy. None of this means that you will not be able to have a good time or let your hair down a bit, but always keep your role as an ambassador for the naval service in mind as you make decisions related to your social and personal conduct.

Hail and Farewells

One of the most common events you will encounter as junior officer is the Hail and Farewell—a social event dedicated to welcoming new additions to the officer community at your command and providing a fitting sendoff for those who are departing. The form and tone of these events vary based on warfare community and individual commands, so take the time to ask a more experienced officer at your command what you should expect.

In its most basic form, the Hail and Farewell begins with an informal meal or light fare, after which the CO welcomes the new additions and their significant others, and the wardroom recognizes those who are leaving. This recognition can take the form of sincere appreciation, gentle ribbing, or a downright roast; make sure you understand what the custom is at your command and recognize that as a new person with limited time you will likely not be expected to make many remarks.

If you are bringing your spouse or a guest to the event, be sure to introduce that person to some of the other officers and guests. If spouses and other guests are included, make an extra effort to keep any remarks or gifts tasteful. These events are among the primary ways wardrooms bond outside the command, but misreading the climate or inadvertently hurting someone's feelings with a comment that was intended to be funny is a pitfall to avoid.

Thank-You Notes

Writing letters and notes has become a bit of a lost art with the advent of e-mail, but thank-you notes are a social custom that has not been replaced with an electronic substitute just yet. If a senior officer has hosted you for dinner, it is always appropriate to thank the host for his or her efforts with a note of thanks. These notes do not have to be long, but they should be sincere and specific so they do not read like a form letter. Remember to pick a thank-you note card that is both an appropriate representative of who you are and suitable for the person receiving it. A white or cream note card with your initials or a conservative picture on the front would be a good choice if you have never shopped for stationery before. Regardless, sending a note of thanks to someone who has hosted you for a meal or been kind to you in another way is a courtesy that will never go out of style.

Civilian Clothing

Just as you want to be in the right uniform at a military event, we all feel our best when we are dressed appropriately in street clothes as well. If you have not had a chance to purchase a suit yet, this is probably the right time to do so. A conservative dark suit for more formal events and a good-quality blue blazer for less formal occasions are good additions for a young male officer's wardrobe. Female officers should look to buy clothing appropriate for more formal events as well—a pantsuit and a versatile dress that you can accessorize would be good and useful choices. These purchases will likely represent a substantial expense in light of a young officer's limited budget, but remember that a few high-quality, conservatively styled items will provide you with the best return on your clothing investment over the long run.

While khakis and a polo shirt or button-down for men and dress slacks or a skirt for women will be the right choice for the vast majority of your events, there will times when having a suit or blazer available will allow you to more comfortably participate in a social event. In many other parts of the world dining can be more formal, and wearing a sport coat or nicer dress will allow you to blend in. If you are in a command that deploys, you will definitely want to bring a civilian suit or blazer, or the appropriate equivalent for women, along with your less formal liberty attire.

Events in more conservative regions of the world may require women to wear a shawl or jacket over a sleeveless outfit. Additionally, you may be invited to an optional event or two that requires nicer clothing. Opportunities to dine with local dignitaries or business leaders are often very positive, memorable experiences that you will not want to miss because you left your sport coat or nice dress at home prior to deployment.

Regardless of where you are going, represent the Navy well. Never wear ripped, suggestive, or revealing clothing; and although flip-flops are fine at a beach party, they may not be appropriate for your first wardroom function at the CO's house.

Introductions

The Navy is not overly formal regarding introductions in general, but most naval leaders will expect you to introduce yourself and the person accompanying you to an event—they are looking forward to meeting you! Because this is such a standard custom, you will quickly find yourself becoming very comfortable with introductions, and you can expect to assimilate much more quickly into a social setting than you would in a civilian environment.

The mechanics of a simple introduction are not difficult. A simple, "Commander Jones, I would like to introduce you to my friend, John Smith," works just fine. The general rules of introductions are that a junior person is introduced to a senior, a younger person to someone older, and, if seniority is not an issue, females are introduced to males. If you remember to mention the senior person first, the rest of the introduction is easy—"Admiral Smith, I would like you to meet my wife, Katherine Jackson."

Tipping

While the standard tip for a waiter is 15–20 percent for a sit-down meal in the United States, there are a number of other services where a tip is often expected. At hotels, it is customary to tip bellhops one to two dollars per bag, with the same going to skycaps if they help you with your bags at the airport. Unlike civilian food stores, baggers at the commissary (the on-base grocery store) are often paid largely from small tips. For barbershops and beauty shops both on base and off base, tipping customs are relatively similar—15–20 percent of the price of the service. For taxi drivers, tip 15 percent of the overall fare.

Internationally, tipping customs vary widely, so it is worth checking with those who have lived in country for a while or refer to a good travel book. If you are part of a deployed command, you are likely to receive an entering port brief at which a fleet liaison will discuss local customs. Those briefing you will be an excellent source of advice on tipping and other social customs in the country.

Conclusion

By showing consideration, respect, and consistency in the way you approach your social interactions you are creating a framework that will enhance your ability to engage others and be comfortable and confident. Most officers find the naval profession's code of social ethics to be one of the best features of naval life, and one that creates a foundation for friendships that can last a lifetime. Although this small chapter will not make you a protocol expert, remembering the watchwords "consideration," "respect," and "consistency" will serve you well as you embark on your naval career.

5

Leave, Liberty, and Travel

Leave and liberty are subjects near and dear to every Sailor's heart, and they will be to yours, too. The old recruiting slogan "Join the Navy and see the world" is often quite true, and even in this age of heightened force protection, the opportunity to travel is still a very attractive feature of the naval profession. Regardless of your next destination, it will be worthwhile to review the Navy's policies on leave, liberty, and travel so you can manage your own travel and monitor the liberty and leave of your Sailors.

Leave

All service members have a right to annual leave. Leave is a formally granted paid vacation that will be interrupted only in extraordinary circumstances. You will accumulate 2.5 days of leave per month of active service (30 days per year), and as of 2018 you can carry a maximum of 60 days across a fiscal year. In other words, if you had 75 days of unused leave on the books on 1 October, you would lose 15 of those days and would begin accumulating 2.5 days per month again until the next fiscal year. Some Sailors may meet special criteria to carry more than sixty days of leave each year and may be entitled to "special leave accrual" (SLA). More information about the Navy's leave policy and SLA policy can be found in MILPERSMAN 1050-010 and MILPERSMAN 1050-070. Of course, if you regularly use your leave, you will keep the total accumulated number of days below sixty at the end of the fiscal year and will never lose any.

Under exceptional circumstances, such as a family emergency, leave that puts you in a negative leave balance state will be granted as long as you have enough obligated service left to "work off" the negative leave balance at the rate of 2.5 days per month, but this exception is managed very carefully.

Leave requests are made through an electronic system called Navy Standard Integrated Personnel System (NSIPS) and routed through your chain of command for approval. On board a ship, your chain of command may include the section leader, fire marshal, command duty officer, watchbill coordinator, department head, executive officer, and finally the commanding officer, so except in an emergency, route your leave request well in advance.

While all commands utilize NSIPS to track leave electronically, some commands may still require routing hard-copy leave chits. Once approved, the admin department will enter the approved leave dates into NSIPS. Although NSIPS contains an automatic check-in and check-out function, some commands may also require the command duty officer, OOD, or admin officer to sign your hard-copy leave papers, indicating the date and time you actually checked out on leave and returned. If your command does not require paper leave chits, you should print and carry your approved electronic chit from NSIPS before starting your leave. If you are traveling by air, your flight might be canceled, and you might need to use your leave chit as leverage to get on the next available return flight.

Emergency leave is granted under special circumstances such as the illness or death of an immediate family member. An important point, however, is that emergency leave is not free; it will still be charged against your leave balance. But it sometimes offers benefits such as priority placement on military transportation or reduced prices on commercial airline tickets.

Liberty

Liberty is the time you have after work until the start of the next workday. In the Navy this will vary with workload and operational schedule. You can expect to be granted liberty at the end of a normal workday unless you have duty. Being on liberty does not mean you are free from the Navy's regulations and expectations; you are *always* subject to the rules and regulations of the Navy and your command.

Liberty for enlisted Sailors is often a more formal process. Most at-sea commands observe set work hours and muster times, but officers often have a little

While Sailors may join the Navy to see the world, Navy leaders also make it a better place. Here ENS James Zumwalt makes a drawing for a child living in an orphanage in Vietnam.
U.S. Navy, MC2 John Beeman

more latitude in managing their own liberty. Despite this extra flexibility, you will be expected to be ready and prepared for officers' call and quarters in the morning, and your own self-imposed schedule will be usually far more demanding than anything formally published in the plan of the day.

Travel

During your career you will likely travel in an official capacity both individually and as part of a group. You will also be able to take advantage of various opportunities to travel in an unofficial capacity on military transport for personal leisure.

Official Travel

Much of the traveling you will do in your naval career will be defined as temporary additional duty, universally known as TAD (or TDY). In your first few years of service, your most likely form of TAD will be for schools and instruction lasting less than six months. You may be required to travel individually or in small groups in support of your command's mission (attending conferences, visiting subunits, cross-training, and visiting sites in industry). Travel in this case may be on military aircraft and vehicles, or you may be issued a commercial airline ticket. In either case you will be entitled to certain monetary allowances, which you will receive after filing a travel claim, described below.

Travel allowances. The Joint Federal Travel Regulations (JFTR) govern all DoD-related travel. Usually you can expect to be paid a per-diem rate sufficient to pay for accommodations and meals when on TAD travel. You will also be reimbursed for certain other expenses such as tolls and taxies if they are accrued in the course of official business. If you travel by commercial air you may be entitled to a rental car, but be sure this is spelled out on your orders before you rent one.

Frequent travelers are issued a government-provided credit card to secure lodging, pay for meals and car rental (if it has been preapproved), and so on. Misuse of government credit cards has resulted in very tight restrictions on whom the cards can be issued to and what they can be used to purchase. If you are curious, you can dig further into the JFTR at http://www.defensetravel.dod.mil/Docs/perdiem/JTR.pdf; otherwise, talk to your admin office about exactly what you are entitled to.

Travel claims. After completion of travel you will need to submit a travel claim to your admin office to be reimbursed for your expenses. After your local personnel support detachment (PSD) processes your claim, the appropriate sum of money will be deposited directly into your bank account. After an extended period of travel, such as during a permanent change of station (PCS) move for you and your family, submitting a travel claim can be fairly complicated. Be sure to keep all of your receipts for lodging, rental cars, plane tickets, and any other expenses exceeding seventy-five dollars.

Traveling in uniform. When traveling within the United States you may be required to travel in uniform if you are part of a command-sponsored group. During most domestic travel situations, wearing civilian clothes will be the more practical choice. If you do travel in uniform, you will usually be in the uniform of the day (either dress blues or summer whites), but CNT "dress" khakis are also acceptable. Outside the United States you will always be required to wear civilian clothes when using commercial transportation, for force-protection reasons. If you are flying on a military transport, you may be required to wear a uniform; make sure you check ahead with the military air terminal you will be departing from.

Unofficial Travel

Aside from normal leave and liberty, one of the great benefits of military life is the chance it gives you to explore the world beyond the United States. Your ship or squadron may visit overseas locations, or you may simply decide to take advantage of a military transport "hop" for leave in an international city or tourist destination.

Travel associated with normal leave and liberty within the United States. Every service member is entitled to leave and liberty, and you will no doubt want to take advantage of the opportunity to travel away from your home port or base. There are a few rules you should keep in mind. Any absence outside normal working hours usually requires an approved "special request" chit. An absence greater than ninety-six hours will require taking formal leave.

In addition to these general rules, local commands may have restrictions on how far you can travel from home base without submitting a special request chit or leave papers. Check with your department head on this issue. The section below on managing your division's leave and liberty presents some considerations for safe travel that apply equally to your Sailors and to you—always keep in mind that in almost every year in recent history, more Sailors are killed or injured on leave and liberty than at work.

Overseas travel. If you plan to travel overseas, you will generally need to submit a leave request. It is also a good idea to give an itinerary and list of contact numbers to your department head before you depart so he or she can track you down if needed. Many local commanders overseas have rules on the minimum size of a travel party ("buddy rules") and a detailed list of off-limits locations. Check with your antiterrorism/force protection officer to see if any of these rules apply or if you need to be briefed on the local terrorism threat (the more "exotic" the location you intend to visit, the more likely you will need to complete a training session). In many cases you will be required to prepare an individual force protection and travel plan even if your travel is for pleasure.

Just as when you are at home, you are a representative of both your country and the Navy when you travel abroad. Respect local customs, dress and act appropriately, and avoid confrontations with the locals. If you do find yourself in trouble, contact your command and the nearest U.S. military facility or U.S. embassy/consulate as soon as possible.

Space-A travel. As a member of the military you are entitled to take advantage of military air transport for free (or nearly free) travel. It's a terrific way to use your off-duty time to see the world. For the most part, this means using the formal Air Force Air Mobility Command (AMC) Space Available system. A word of caution: "space available" means exactly that. If there is a seat available on an aircraft bound for your destination, you will get it, but if a higher-priority passenger shows up just before departure, you could find yourself scrambling to find alternative (and expensive) transportation. Aircraft may also be diverted or delayed with no notice. Always give yourself a time cushion when traveling Space-A, and make sure you have an alternative way home if the worst happens. For more on using AMC Space-A, take a look at these websites:

- Air Mobility Command, http://www.amc.af.mil/Home/AMC-Travel-Site/
- NAS Norfolk Passenger Terminal, https://www.facebook.com/NorfolkPassengerTerminal/
- NAS North Island Passenger Terminal, https://www.facebook.com/NASNorthIsland.AirTerminal/

Managing Your Division's Leave and Liberty

Leave and liberty are subjects that loom large in the daily life of your Sailors. You will be faced with many requests for special liberty and leave that you will have to balance against workload, operations, and command policy. A good leader knows when to say "no." The flip side of this coin is that a good leader should also know when to advocate for a request that warrants approval. This section presents some tips on how to handle your division's time off.

Normal Leave

Normal leave generally falls into one of two categories: command-wide stand-down periods and individual leave. Command-wide stand-down leave will occur on a designated period over a holiday or before or after a deployment. The usual practice is to divide the stand-down period in half and allow the crew to take leave during one half or the other. Your job here is to make sure that there are enough people during each period to carry on with routine work and man watches (making a chart listing each member of your division down the side and the dates they will take leave across the top is one useful way to visualize the situation). Remember to keep an eye on your Sailors' leave balance, and be cautious about allowing someone to attain a negative leave balance. Finally, you will inevitably have to deal with requests that do not match up with designated leave periods. These requests may not merit an automatic "no" but must be viewed in context with the ship's needs and fairness to your other Sailors.

Individual leave can often require a little more skill to manage. Operational commands normally permit 10 percent of an organization to take leave during normal in-port periods. Before checking the "yes" box and routing the chit up the chain of command, you must consider your division's workload, the command's operational schedule, the member's leave balance, and command policies. You will also have to consider if the leave applicant has a unique or critical skill that the command cannot afford to lose for that period of time. No one can tell you how to adjudicate every case, but you must balance the individual's needs against the impact on your division and the command and be prepared to articulate your decision. If you recommend disapproval, you must still route the chit up the chain of command to the CO, because only he or she has the authority to disapprove any leave request.

Emergency Leave

Many of the same considerations for ordinary leave apply to the decision to grant emergency leave, but the decision should be biased in favor of the individual's needs if he or she meets the criteria for emergency leave. It will be a rare circumstance where leave is not granted in the case of a genuine emergency involving the immediate family of one of your Sailors. Of course, what constitutes a "genuine emergency" is often in the eye of the beholder—you will no doubt experience situations during your career where you doubt if the "emergency" in question really merits granting leave, especially if your unit is deployed overseas. In these gray areas, seek the advice of your chief or department head.

One way to confirm that an emergency is genuine is to request an AMCROSS message. The American Red Cross works closely with all military bases by helping to confirm emergencies (often by consulting with a physician) and transmitting a message or calling the command directly. Most medical facilities that deal with military patients will be familiar with this process, but in some cases you may need to have the Sailor contact a family member on the scene to get things rolling. Another valuable resource in this case is the command ombudsman, who is specifically trained to deal with such situations.

Coincident with processing the emergency leave request, you will need to ensure that adequate travel arrangements are made and that the Sailor has sufficient funds to get home. Consult with your command master chief (CMC) on this issue—many commands have a small emergency fund or can expedite processing of a loan from the Navy–Marine Corps Relief Society. For more on Navy Relief, which assists service members in need with loans and grants, see the Navy–Marine Corps Relief Society website: www.nmcrs.org.

Liberty

As a general rule, you should seek to provide the daily time off for your Sailors that is consistent with your command's liberty policies. While you never want to hold them on the ship or at work unnecessarily, you will want to balance the notion of maximizing liberty with the need to do more than merely complete the minimum work necessary to keep your organization afloat.

One thing that will quickly be apparent to you is that there is always something to do in the Navy. All of us value our free time, but you must always keep mission accomplishment uppermost in your mind. Your command may or may not have a strict policy on liberty hours; if not, talk this issue over with your chief and your department head. No matter what the policy, you must be prepared to manage liberty appropriately to meet an often challenging workload. As always, keep your boss informed.

Depending on the operational tempo of your command, there may be times where your Sailors will desire liberty during the day to take care of a particular need or to participate in an event such as serving as a class parent. While your chief and you will certainly want to support worthwhile requests if your command schedule allows it, you will also want make sure that your Sailors are not habitually asking for time off during the workday to accomplish things they could do on their own time. Like many leadership experiences, these decisions require a sense of balance between the needs of your Sailors and the needs of your command.

Liberty normally expires in the morning around 0700, at which time your division will turn in a muster report accounting for all hands. Sometimes—especially when overseas—liberty will expire at an unusual time, such as midnight. In these cases, good division officers will be up and about to make sure everybody in their divisions have made it back to the ship on time and in good shape.

Special Liberty
Special liberty is granted for specific reasons during normal working hours for periods of twenty-four to ninety-six hours. It is approved through the process of routing a special request chit up the chain of command. Local policies vary, but most units give division officers authority to grant up to twenty-four hours of special liberty, while longer periods (up to a maximum of ninety-six hours) must be granted further up the chain. As with all special requests, any chit that is marked "no" must go all the way up the chain of command for final disposition.

Safety Considerations
Motor vehicle accidents are the leading cause of death and serious injury in the Navy. Most leave and liberty involve travel, often over long distances in varying weather. As a good division officer you should pay close attention to your people's travel plans and spend some time talking about making smart choices. You should also consider vehicle safety inspections and requiring a "trip plan," especially for your younger Sailors. The Navy Safety Center website has examples of vehicle inspection check sheets, trip plans, and a host of tips on driver and travel safety: http://www.public.navy.mil/NAVSAFECEN/Pages/index.aspx.

Conclusion
Leave and liberty are vital to your well-being and that of your Sailors. As a newly commissioned officer you will spend a considerable amount of your energy managing leave and liberty for the Sailors who work for you. On occasion you will have to make some hard calls while trying to balance the needs of individual Sailors with broader mission accomplishment. Make sure you understand local policies, communicate with your boss, and always be honest with your Sailors. Even though you will not be able to make every single Sailor happy every time, taking the steps outlined in this chapter will put you well on your way to consistently managing this important aspect of naval life.

6

Pay and Benefits

The Navy is a large, complex organization, so a review of the structure of naval pay and benefits may be helpful. In addition to understanding your own compensation, as a leader you will also need to be equipped to provide counsel to your Sailors when they need it.

Pay

Your monthly paycheck—which includes basic pay, special pays, and allowances—is disbursed to your bank account twice a month, in two relatively equal amounts. You will also receive various one-time disbursements for things such as travel and moving expenses. Finally, most officers will receive periodic bonuses for committing to further service. This section briefly discusses each of these pay types to get you oriented and provides some websites where you can find further information.

Basic Pay

Basic pay is set by law based on your pay grade (rank) and years of service. You will receive a pay raise when you are promoted and with every two years of completed service. Each year, Congress adjusts the pay tables with an across-the-board raise to account for inflation (often around 2–3 percent) and may target certain pay grades for slightly higher raises to influence retention. Currently, the officer pay table runs from zero to forty years of service and from pay grades

O-1 (ensign) to O-10 (admiral). The web address below will take you to the current pay table at the Defense Finance Accounting Service (DFAS) military pay site. Click on "Military Pay Tables," then go to the year you are looking for: https://www.dfas.mil/militarymembers/payentitlements/military-pay-charts.html.

Special Pays

Special pays come in many varieties. Some of the most common include sea pay, flight pay, and submarine pay. Flight pay and submarine pay are for aircraft crewmembers and officers assigned to submarine duty respectively. Officers assigned to seagoing commands are eligible for sea pay. Imminent danger pay is for service in designated geographic regions such as the Middle East, and personnel involved in certain hazardous activities such as flight deck operations receive hazardous duty pay. Dollar amounts for each of these pays are available for the current fiscal year at the website cited above. For detailed eligibility requirements you may consult the DoD comptroller's site: https://www.dfas.mil/militarymembers/payentitlements/specialpay.html.

For a user-friendly explanation of special pays, visit one of the commercial websites that cater to the military, such as www.military.com or www.militarytimes.com. As always, when it comes to pay, talk to your disbursing officer or local PSD if you have questions.

Allowances

The final part of your monthly paycheck is made up of various allowances. Officers receive a basic allowance for subsistence (BAS) to pay for meals (note that officers pay for their meals even while assigned to a ship) and a family separation allowance (FSA) while deployed, if they have dependents. Basic allowance for housing (BAH) covers housing costs and varies depending on location, pay grade, and marital status. BAH charts for each geographic area are available at the website below by typing in the zip code of the area you are interested in: https://www.defensetravel.dod.mil/site/bahCalc.cfm.

Bonus Pay

Most officers who choose to serve past their initial service obligation receive an annual bonus in exchange for agreeing to continue to serve. In the case of nuclear power officers and special warfare officers, these bonuses can be substantial. Rules vary greatly by community, so talk to a mentor or your detailer for specifics. Skimming the Bureau of Naval Personnel (BUPERS) website for your officer community may also yield some answers: http://www.npc.navy.mil/Officer/.

Taxation

Not all of your pay is taxable. The rule of thumb is that compensation that has "pay" in its name is taxable, and anything that is an "allowance" is nontaxable. Another nuance is that pay received in a war or "hazardous" zone is nontaxable up to a certain amount. The nontaxable-portion rule is rather complicated for officers. Any pay above what the senior master chief in the Navy (an E-9 with more than forty years of service on the pay chart) would receive is taxable.

Bonus payments are taxed based on the month you receive them, so they would be fully taxed under normal circumstances and only taxed beyond an E-9's pay if they are received while serving in a combat zone. The DoD determines the areas that qualify as "tax free," and eligibility is based on the member spending at least one day of any given month in a designated zone. For example, the waters of the Persian Gulf are a tax-free area. The supply officer or disbursing officer at your command will be well versed in these issues if you have any questions.

Managing Your Pay

The Navy allows service members to manage certain aspects of their pay through a DFAS-supported website known as MyPay. The MyPay site allows you to view your monthly leave and earnings statement (LES), which gives a detailed account of all monthly pays, deductions (for things such as taxes and allotments), and your accumulated leave days. You should examine your LES monthly, especially if you note an unexpected increase or decrease in pay. Other functions available on the MyPay site include the following:

- Starting, stopping, or modifying a savings allotment or a monthly allotment to a dependent
- Setting up or modifying the account where your pay is deposited (direct deposit)

- Changing your federal or state tax withholding status
- Obtaining a copy of your annual W-2 form
- Viewing the allotment of monthly pay to the Thrift Savings Plan (more on TSP later)
- Tracking the disposition of any travel claims you have submitted in the last 180 days

The MyPay site is password protected. You can sign up at https://mypay.dfas.mil/mypay.aspx.

If you run into problems with your pay (not unheard of in the naval service), talk to your local PSD or to the command PSD liaison representative (PLR). If you have to work directly with PSD, your command should have a designated customer service representative to help you, but quite often you can resolve problems through the PLR in your unit's admin office.

Pay and Your Sailors

In your role as a leader you will encounter Sailors with a wide range of financial backgrounds and knowledge, running the gamut from those with a significant portfolio and a solid investment plan to the newly married eighteen-year-old who has never filed a tax return or learned to balance a checkbook. Those who are most vulnerable often fall prey to easy credit scams and unscrupulous lenders, and the Navy spends considerable time trying to equip its Sailors with the knowledge to avoid these traps. You will play a significant role in these efforts, and when problems do occur, you will need to be involved.

The Servicemembers Civil Relief Act of 2003 has reduced the prevalence of these unfair lending practices, but it is always a good idea to discuss these issues with your Sailors regularly to help them avoid financial pitfalls. This is especially important for Sailors in technical ratings. Uncontrolled and unpaid debts can prevent Sailors from obtaining or maintaining access to classified information.

Guiding Your Sailors

A little advance effort can go a long way toward helping your Sailors avoid financial problems. Take the time to talk informally to your troops about making smart financial decisions and avoiding the dangers of too much debt. Also, consider scheduling formal divisional training using the command financial specialist (CFS) or outside experts to provide instruction. Younger Sailors or those who appear to be headed toward financial trouble can be directed to one-on-one counseling with the CFS or at the local Fleet and Family Support Center (FFSC).

The FFSC in each U.S. Navy home port provides excellent financial counseling geared both to aiding individuals in trouble and to helping Sailors and their families build a secure financial future. In addition to providing individual counseling, each FFSC periodically offers free classes on such subjects as the dangers of payday loans and easy credit, car-buying strategies, retirement planning, savings and investments, and identity theft awareness. Below is the main website for the FFSC, but search for the site associated with your local FFSC to get class details and contact numbers: https://www.cnic.navy.mil/ffr/family_readiness/fleet_and_family_support_program.html.

Sailors in Financial Distress

Financial burdens can impact the day-to-day performance of Sailors and in extreme cases can result in a loss of security clearances and can drive vulnerable Sailors to poor financial and ethical decisions. While cases as extreme as this are relatively rare, a chain of command can expend considerable time and effort dealing with personal financial problems. When you become aware of a Sailor experiencing financial distress, first talk to the Sailor's chief and then inform your boss. How involved you and the chain of command become depends on the nature of the problem and the competence of the individual. Remember to use the CFS (and possibly counselors at the FFSC) to help the service member. The local chapter of the Navy–Marine Corps Relief Society also offers budgeting assistance and no-interest loans for Sailors in financial difficulty: http://www.nmcrs.org.

Benefits

When you joined the Navy you became entitled to an enviable number of benefits. This section briefly describes them and gives web addresses where you can explore them further.

Medical and Dental Care

As a service member you have ready access to Navy-provided medical and dental care. This is relatively straightforward, but care for your dependents is a bit more complicated. Your dependents will obtain healthcare through Tricare, the military's health management system. When enrolling in Tricare, your dependent will select one of the following options for care, as quoted from the Tricare website:

- Tricare Prime is a managed care option similar to a civilian health maintenance organization (HMO). Active duty members and their families do not pay enrollment fees, annual deductibles, or copayments for care in the TRICARE network.
- Tricare Select is a self-managed, fee-for-service preferred provider network option available to active duty family members. Members can visit any Tricare-authorized provider for medically necessary services covered by Tricare without a referral. You'll pay a copay or cost share based on the type of care and type of provider you see (network vs. non-network).

For more information, go to https://www.tricare.mil.

Tricare also administers a dental insurance program for dependents that covers limited dental work for a small monthly fee. More information is available at https://tricare.mil/CoveredServices/Dental/TDP.

Life Insurance

Navy members are automatically enrolled into the Servicemembers' Group Life Insurance (SGLI) program unless they specifically decline coverage. As of 2018 the maximum coverage is $400,000 for a monthly fee of $29 (which will be automatically deducted from your pay). Be sure that you update not only your "Page 2" at the admin office but also your SGLI Election and Certificate form with the correct beneficiary information at the SGLI Online Enrollment System (SOES). The Department of Veterans Affairs (which administers SGLI) website has more information on SGLI as well as other veterans' benefits: https://benefits.va.gov/insurance/sgli.asp#cover.

Thrift Savings Plan

The TSP allows uniformed service members to contribute a certain percentage of their pay to a defined benefits retirement plan that offers many of the same tax and savings benefits of a civilian 401k. Briefly, you may contribute

The Navy works to invest in its people and their families through pay, medical care, and a variety of other benefits.
U.S. Navy, JOSN Brandon Shelander

an amount up to the annual limit ($18,500 as of 2018) to a number of managed investment funds, deferring the tax on the contribution until withdrawal (presumably in retirement, when your income tax rate will be much lower). For further details, see the uniformed service TSP website (https://www.tsp.gov/index.html) or talk to your command financial specialist.

Tuition Assistance

Most warfare communities want their commissioned officers to obtain a master's degree sometime after their initial tour. Options include the Naval Postgraduate School, the Naval War College, an assortment of fellowships, and various community-specific programs such as the Surface Warfare Officer Graduate Education Voucher. For specifics on these programs, see the BUPERS graduate education website at http://www.public.navy.mil/bupers-npc/career/education/Pages/default.aspx.

Many officers, however, choose to pursue advanced degrees on their own time. Tuition assistance (TA) is available to offset the costs for continuing education at almost any accredited institution. As of 2018 TA pays a maximum of $250 per semester hour, up to sixteen semester hours per fiscal year. Keep in mind that any officer who uses TA incurs a two-year service obligation, which is served concurrently with any other obligation (in other words, the obligation is not tacked on to the end of any other obligation you may have, but you will have to serve a minimum of two years from the time you accept TA). For more on TA, visit https://www.navycollege.navy.mil/tuition-assistance/index.htm.

Family Support Programs

The Fleet and Family Support Center in your home port has a wide assortment of programs available to help you and your family. These include the following:

- Financial planning assistance—classes and one-on-one counseling
- Relocation services—help with planning your transfer
- New parent support—education for new and soon-to-be parents
- Family employment—assistance with résumé preparation, interview skill building, and job searches for dependents
- Deployment support—tips and support for families of service members approaching and on deployment

The FFSC also provides command support in cases involving domestic violence and sexual assault. The main FFSC website is listed here, but you should also search for the local FFSC in your home port: https://www.cnic.navy.mil/ffr/family_readiness/fleet_and_family_support_program.html.

VA Home Loan Benefit

Another benefit you should be aware of is the VA home loan guarantee. As a service member you are entitled to a loan guarantee from the Veterans Administration that can help you get approved for a home loan and may significantly lower the interest rate you can obtain. For more information, visit the VA home loan site: https://www.benefits.va.gov/homeloans/.

Getting Financially Smart—For You and Your Sailors

The Navy's pay and benefit system can seem quite complex, but understanding your compensation will ensure that you are not incurring unnecessary expenses by paying for benefits that are already provided. More important, by understanding your compensation you will be more prepared to help your Sailors should they have financial questions or encounter difficulties. Take some time to visit the websites listed in this chapter and become comfortable with the terminology and your entitlements. Doing so will not only help you navigate your finances during your first years in the Navy, it will also profit the Sailors you lead.

7

Understanding U.S. Navy Programs and Policies

As an organization strongly defined by its integrity and values, the U.S. Navy places a great deal of emphasis on the conduct, welfare, and employment of its people. Despite the sophisticated technology and tactics we employ, the Navy is a "people" business. As a newly commissioned officer, part of your role as a leader and manager of your Sailors will depend on your grasp of a wide variety of important programs and policies that support our Sailors. This chapter provides some insight into the programs and policies that the U.S. Navy uses to help Sailors accomplish the mission.

While it is impossible to review every program or instruction that touches the lives of your Sailors, we will begin with the core values that guide our decision making and management. Then we will move on to how leadership sets the course for our work. Finally, we will spend a large portion of the chapter looking at how the Navy helps us work together to support our families.

The U.S. Navy's Core Values

Honor, courage, commitment. These are the Navy's core values, and they are the bedrock that forms the foundation of our service. As a newly commissioned officer you are called to embody these characteristics and provide a role model for your Sailors to emulate. This is not an easy task because you will be making decisions under pressure, in a fast-moving environment, and with the potential to take men and women into harm's way. Even when you find yourself in an environment of relatively lower operational tempo and risk, your ethical decisions will signal to everyone around you how you can be counted on when there are tough decisions to be made.

The Core Values Charter was developed to provide a more complete understanding of the Navy's interpretation of these fundamental building blocks; it is maintained on the Internet homepages of the Navy and Marine Corps. The charter provides the following synopsis of the Navy's core values:

> *Honor.* I am accountable for my professional and personal behavior. I will be mindful of the privilege I have to serve my fellow Americans.
> *Courage.* Courage is the value that gives me the moral and mental strength to do what is right, with confidence and resolution, even in the face of temptation or adversity.
> *Commitment.* The day-to-day duty of every man and woman in the Department of the Navy is to join together as a team to improve the quality of our work, our people, and ourselves.

The Navy is committed to creating an environment in which every leader has the chance to excel and grow.
U.S. Navy, PHC Chris Desmond

Many of your Sailors and fellow officers lived within the ethical framework of these values prior to joining the Navy. For others, these values provide a departure from the life and difficulties they experienced prior to recruit training. Along with the senior enlisted who are your leadership partners, two of your roles as an officer are to ensure that your people are developing these values for themselves and to promote that growth. While describing how you build an ethical organizational climate is no easy task, you will never go wrong by setting the example in your personal conduct and signaling early that you will hold your team to the highest standards.

Understanding How and Why Naval Leaders Share Their Vision

After laying a general cultural foundation, one of the next tasks for leaders is to provide broad direction to their workforce on what the mission is and how it should be accomplished. Vision statements take many forms, and it is not always easy to grasp how service-wide concepts and policies translate to those "close to the deckplates." Although your Sailors will be learning the technical and tactical skills they require to perform their roles, they will often look to you and your CPO to connect what they are doing to the big picture. Your success in this endeavor will depend on your taking the time to learn about and eventually communicate broad naval policies and goals to the men and women who work for you.

Fortunately, our Navy's senior leadership has distilled broader policy into documents that command leadership can use to share the Navy's mission, goals, and direction. A few examples of policy documents and sources you may find useful follow.

- *A Design for Maintaining Maritime Superiority.* Released in January 2016 by the CNO, ADM John M. Richardson, *A Design for Maintaining Maritime Superiority* focuses on two central themes. The first details the Navy's response to evolving strategic and security environments utilizing four main lines of efforts: strengthening naval power at and from sea, achieving high-velocity learning at every level, strengthening our Navy team for the future, and expanding and strengthening our network of partners. Additionally, the design also describes four

core attributes all Sailors should aspire to as the Navy faces twenty-first-century challenges: integrity, accountability, initiative, and toughness.
- The New Maritime Strategy. The CNO and the Commandants of the U.S. Marine Corps and U.S. Coast Guard presented *A Cooperative Strategy for 21st Century Seapower* at the International Seapower Symposium in Newport, Rhode Island, in October 2007. This strategy applied maritime power to the critical protection of America's vital interests in an increasingly interconnected and uncertain world. Revised in 2015, the updated strategy describes how the services would design, organize, and employ assets following new strategic guidance, the ever-changing global security environment, and acknowledging the fiscal constraints the services face.
- Your commanding officer's command philosophy. Most commanding officers publish their intentions for the leadership and management of their command in a short document. This is an especially good way to get a feel for the leadership style of a new CO.
- The U.S. Naval Institute *Proceedings*. This independent professional journal is published monthly. It is often the first place to find major strategy papers from the CNO's staff, but it is also a great resource to determine the role of your command in supporting a specific mission or theater of operations.
- The U.S. Navy website. This site (www.navy.mil) includes a multitude of policy guidance information including the New Maritime Strategy, Sea Power 21, and the CNO's Annual Guidance to the Navy (also referred as CNOG—CNO's Guidance—and a good document to review every year). The Navy website also features news updates, speeches from our leaders, and information sheets that will be immensely helpful to new officers looking to learn about the broader Navy.

Creating a Working Environment Based on Mutual Support and Respect

The Navy has a number of programs in place to ensure that we enjoy a workplace that gives each of us the chance to contribute to the mission and succeed without fear of discrimination or harassment. Human relationships are not always easily bound by written instructions, but your knowledge of these policies and commitment to the ideals behind them are essential to creating a command climate that allows all of your Sailors the chance to serve honorably.

Protecting Equal Opportunity, Preventing Sexual Harassment

Equal Opportunity (EO) is a program that ensures every member of a command has the opportunity to succeed without facing discrimination due to race, ethnicity, national origin, gender, or religion. The perception within a command that some Sailors are being discriminated against based on attributes beyond their control will be devastating to a command's morale and runs counter to the Navy's core values. The instruction that guides our Navy's approach to equal opportunity for all is OPNAVINST 5354.1 series.

Every command is required to have a command managed equal opportunity (CMEO) manager who is the single point of contact for EO issues and who coordinates all complaint reports and resolutions. Should you ever be presented with a situation that is an EO violation or simply raises a question in your mind about EO, the CMEO manager is a person you should interact with at the first opportunity. Understand that your people will watch your reaction to a situation that is or borders on an EO violation. Like all standards, what you let pass without comment or action will become the new level of acceptable behavior, so be vigilant in your efforts to address equal opportunity violations and concerns.

Both the EO policy and the sexual harassment policy (SECNAVINST 5300.26D) provide guidance to prevent and stop sexual harassment. They broadly define what behavior is acceptable, borderline, and unacceptable. These same instructions delineate the process for reporting and addressing EO and sexual harassment issues. The instructions utilize a "reasonable person" standard to determine if sexual harassment has occurred, but recognizing the human dimension involved in this approach, you should avoid conversations, e-mails, or web-based environments that include content of a sexual nature, just as you would in most civilian work environments.

The key to handling reports of sexual harassment is to deal with them honestly, quickly, and in accordance with the Navy's policies. Like many problems you will face in the Navy and in life, failing to respond promptly and properly to sexual harassment will almost always make the problem worse. Sexual harassment issues should be handled at the lowest appropriate level based on the specifics of the individual case.

Based on the severity of the issue or your inability to resolve it, inform the CMEO manager for formal action. Sexual harassment is damaging to a command's good order, discipline, and morale. As a leader, you play a significant role in setting the proper example and taking quick action on violations of the Navy's EO and sexual harassment guidance.

Sexual Assault Prevention and Response (SAPR) Program
Sexual assault is a criminal act. It runs counter to the Navy's core values and erodes the trust not only of the victim of this crime but of the American people, most of all those who entrust their sons and daughters to our care. Whether the assault occurs at work or at home, is perpetrated by a shipmate or someone else, the event will have a traumatic impact on the victim's life, both personally and professionally. The Navy created the SAPR program to establish a codified process for dealing with these very sensitive situations.

The OPNAVINST 1752.1 series provides the details of this program and defines sexual assault as "intentional sexual contact characterized by the use of force, threats, intimidation, or abuse of authority or when the victim does not or cannot consent. The term includes a broad category of sexual offenses consisting of the following specific UCMJ [Uniform Code of Military Justice] offenses: rape, sexual assault, aggravated sexual contact, abusive sexual contact, forcible sodomy (forced oral or anal sex), or attempts to commit these offenses." An important distinction is that sexual assault and sexual harassment are completely different offenses, and different instructions govern the response to each. Again, sexual assault involves the use of force and is a crime under the UCMJ.

To support and care for the victim, each command is required to have SAPR victim advocates (VAs) who act as an initial support structure for the victim. As a leader, it is important for you to ensure that any Sailor who needs to speak with a SAPR VA is afforded an opportunity to do so without delay. It is also important to know who your command's SAPR representatives are and to ensure that you and the team you lead are receiving periodic SAPR training to include guidance on restricted versus unrestricted reporting.

In addition to the SAPR VAs within each command, the DoD offers a crisis support service for victims of sexual assault. DoD Safe Helpline is available 24/7 worldwide with "click, call, or text" user options for anonymous and confidential support. It can be accessed by logging on to www.safehelpline.org

or by calling 1-877-995-5247, but it does not replace local base and installation sexual assault response coordinator (SARC) or SAPR VA contact information.

Fraternization

OPNAVINST 5370.2 defines "fraternization" as "personal relationships which contravene the customary bounds of acceptable senior-subordinate relationships." Although fraternization is often characterized as a male-female issue, any unduly familiar relationship that fails to respect differences in rank and authority constitutes a violation, even if both people are the same gender. Relationships of a personal nature between officers and enlisted, and senior enlisted (E-7 and above) and junior enlisted (E-6 and below) are prohibited. However, the Navy's policies do allow for inclusive participation in command-sponsored events such as picnics and membership on sports teams.

Relationships that constitute fraternization are prejudicial to good order and discipline and are a danger to the unity and efficiency of a command. The exact point at which a relationship becomes unduly familiar may be difficult to identify, so you will want to be particularly vigilant to prevent a professional relationship from lapsing into a personal one. Keep relationships with your subordinates completely professional and take tactful but decisive action in correcting a subordinate who attempts to draw you toward the gray area of this policy. While you must vigilantly live by the Navy's fraternization policy, do not let a distorted fear of regulations completely isolate you from your Sailors. Common sense and a positive but professional tone with your Sailors will keep you on the right track.

Social Media

Reliance on social media has revolutionized communication throughout our fleet. Websites such as Facebook make it easier for Sailors to connect with their families, even while deployed overseas, and to keep in touch with current and former shipmates. Social media can also provide a means to share important information or to voice personal opinions. While you can find a wide array of information on social media platforms, it is important to exercise good judgment when using these sites.

Before you share anything, think about what you are about to post and the audience you intend to view it. Could what you share be misconstrued? Does it violate operational security (OPSEC)? Are you presenting your own personal views or are you sharing information in an official capacity? Regardless, it is important to understand that when you are logged into a social media platform you still represent the U.S. Navy. Finally, it may seem harmless to connect with Sailors of all ranks over the Internet, but if you mismanage those relationships you can quickly find yourself operating in a gray area and could possibly violate the Navy's fraternization policy (see OPNAVINST 5370.2 series). Social media allows you to directly and immediately connect with people you may or may not know, so it is best to remember that this is another opportunity for you to set the example. The resources listed below can provide more information about the Navy's guidance on social media.

- Online Conduct for the Navy Team—http://navylive.dodlive.mil/onlineconduct/
- Web and Internet-based Capabilities (IbC) Policies—Chief Information Officer, U.S. Department of Defense, http://dodcio.defense.gov/DoD-Web-Policy/
- DoD Internet Services and Internet-Based Capabilities—http://www.esd.whs.mil/Portals/54/Documents/DD/issuances/dodi/855001p.pdf
- Operations Security Policy—OPNAVINST 3432.1A

Supporting Navy Families

It takes a great deal of dedication to maintain the world's finest Navy, and our families play an important role in this effort. Accordingly, the Navy's senior leadership has developed programs and policies to assist families in working through the challenges military families face.

The best resource for guidance in this area is the local Fleet and Family Support Center (FFSC). FFSC provides valuable support to the fleet by counseling Sailors on subjects ranging from parenting skills to marriage counseling and financial management. The center is especially helpful to families with both spouses in the military. The counselors provide direct support to families, and they train senior Sailors and officers to provide counsel to shipmates when direct support from shore facilities is not available.

FFSC also provides training to another key family resource: command ombudsmen. The command ombudsman is the spouse of a member of the command who volunteers to serve as the link between the families and the command. The ombudsman is appointed by the CO and serves the command by listening to the concerns of Sailors' families, keeping them informed on certain aspects of the ship's schedule and operations, and connecting families with support structures that can provide help.

Family Advocacy Program

Just as with sexual abuse, the abuse of a child or spouse is both inexcusable and inconsistent with the Navy's core values. The Family Advocacy Program (FAP) provides clinical assessment, treatment, and services for military members and their families involved in incidents of domestic abuse in order to protect victims from future abuse. The guiding instruction on FAP, SECNAVINST 1752.3B, lists five primary goals for this program:

- Prevention
- Victim safety and protection
- Offender accountability
- Rehabilitative education and counseling
- Community accountability/responsibility for a consistent appropriate response

FAP is a command program and leadership effort that focuses on reducing incidents of child and domestic abuse and getting treatment and care for victims. If you encounter the possibility of child abuse within a Navy family, contact your chain of command and the command's family advocacy representative right away—the unacceptability of child and domestic abuse as well as the related legal and privacy issues warrant an immediate and well-informed response from you and your command.

Personal Readiness

The Navy takes a great deal of interest in the well-being of Sailors in all facets of their lives. While in service to the nation we enjoy complete medical care and the considerable benefits of commissaries and the Navy Exchange. We also are supported by a wide variety of programs that ensure we are healthy and productive citizens and family members.

In the last decade the Navy has taken a more holistic approach to the health and wellness of our Sailors. Staying physically fit, eating right, and getting adequate sleep build resilience and enhance our capacity to make good decisions, solve problems, and perform under pressure.

Physical Readiness

OPNAVINST 611.1J emphasizes the importance of physical fitness, which is "a crucial element of mission performance, particularly those in an operational or crisis environment, and must be a part of every Sailor's life. Mission readiness and operational effectiveness are built on the physical fitness of the individual; therefore, all naval personnel shall maintain personal physical fitness by regular exercise and proper nutrition."

Unfortunately, you may encounter otherwise very effective Sailors who jeopardize their career by their inability to maintain required physical readiness and body fat standards. Make every effort you can to support your Sailors in improving their fitness and ensure that those who struggle to maintain the standards are working closely with the command fitness leader (CFL) to improve their physical condition.

Naval personnel must complete a physical fitness assessment (PFA) on a semiannual basis, although future updates to the program may include incentivized changes. The PFA includes a medical screening, a body composition assessment (BCA), and a physical readiness test (PRT). In rare circumstances, medical waivers may be granted to personnel; however, personnel who receive two consecutive medical waivers or three waivers within a four-year period will be referred to a military treatment facility (MTF) for a medical evaluation board (MEB). Medical waivers do not apply to pregnant servicewomen, who are instead administratively listed in a "pregnancy status" category and are exempt from completing the PRT or BCA (see OPNAVINST 6110.1J).

The BCA is determined utilizing a three-step process: the height and weight standard, a single-site abdominal measurement, and a body circumference measurement. If a Sailor's height and weight exceed what OPNAVIST 6110.1J prescribes, then a single-site abdominal measurement is taken. If the Sailor's single-site abdominal measurement exceeds the standard, then a body circumference measurement is taken. These measurements are used to determine body fat composition. Sailors will fail the BCA portion of the PFA if they do not meet any of the standards employed. Failing the BCA portion of the PFA constitutes an overall PFA failure.

The PRT is a series of physical tests that assess cardio-respiratory fitness, muscular strength, and endurance. Sailors must demonstrate muscular strength in the push-up and sit-up test and cardiovascular condition in the one-and-a-half-mile run. Commanding officers may also authorize stationary bikes, treadmills, or the five-hundred-yard swim as alternate cardiovascular tests, and one or more of these options is available in most commands.

Sailors who fail to meet minimum standards are required to participate in their command's fitness enhancement program to ensure they have an opportunity to improve their physical condition under a structured workout regimen. Any Sailor who fails three or more tests in a four-year span becomes eligible for administrative separation from the Navy.

Nutrition

Proper nutrition is an equal partner in your health regimen and the Navy's fitness program. Over time, poor nutrition can cause an increase in body weight, a decrease in energy levels, and can lead to serious medical conditions that will affect operational readiness. Common poor nutritional decisions include choosing fast food, skipping meals, and consuming empty calories. Lack of energy, poor sleep, and shifting schedules can lead to overuse of energy drinks and supplements, which, ironically, can immediately reduce the body's ability to respond to emergencies. Encourage your Sailors to choose wisely what they eat.

Sleep

Sleep is another crucial element related to building peak personal readiness to train and fight. Recognizing the unique rigors and irregular hours our mission often demands, leaders must safeguard this necessary component of individual readiness. Fatigue has negative effects on readiness, effectiveness, and safety. Adequate sleep not only sharpens performance and increases endurance but also reduces stress, improves productivity, and boosts morale. Many commands have implemented measures to help tackle personnel fatigue, including prioritizing rest periods for their teams, employing circadian watch schedules, and aligning daily routines with watch schedules.

Alcohol and Drug Use

OPNAVINST 5350.4D warns that "drug and alcohol abuse pose a severe threat to a Sailor's combat readiness in terms of performance, reliability, judgment, and time lost. It undermines health, safety, discipline, and loyalty. Drug and alcohol abuse is incompatible with the maintenance of high standards of performance, military discipline, and readiness and is destructive of U.S. Navy efforts to instill pride, promote professionalism, and enhance personal excellence."

The drug and alcohol prevention adviser (DAPA) at your duty station is tasked with assisting the CO in ensuring that all personnel follow the requirements of the Navy's drug and alcohol abuse prevention and control policy (OPNAVINST 5350.4D). The basic tenets of the policy are zero tolerance for drug use and responsible use of alcohol for those of legal age. Any Sailor who is caught or who admits to using illegal drugs of any kind must be processed for separation from the Navy by his or her CO.

The alcohol use policy issues clear guidelines with respect to Sailors who commit "alcohol-related incidents" (ARIs). An ARI is any violation of the UCMJ, including public drunkenness and driving under the influence, committed when, in the judgment of the CO, alcohol was a contributing factor. If the violation is severe, the Sailor is administratively discharged. If the violation is less severe, the Sailor will be directed to attend alcohol abuse treatment coordinated by the DAPA. Should a Sailor have any additional ARIs, he or she will be administratively discharged.

The days when "drinking like a Sailor" and irresponsible behavior while on liberty were tolerated and even expected are long gone. Commands are directed to deglamorize the use of alcohol and apply measures to ensure that all hands are trained on the professional and physical effects of alcohol use and abuse. Command-sponsored events must provide a nonalcoholic beverage option and must strictly prohibit any participation in activities that encourage excessive and irresponsible drinking.

Anyone, including yourself, who has an alcohol-dependence problem should seek help by contacting the DAPA before any disciplinary action is initiated. Such self-referral enables the DAPA to provide the needed treatment without the negative consequences associated with ARIs. For instance, it is not appropriate for evaluators to reference a self-referral in any way on a Sailor's evaluation.

Alcohol use is another area where your on-duty and off-duty behavior will provide examples that support and encourage Sailors to do the same. Junior officers who put themselves in a situation where their Sailors—or their superiors—observe them abusing alcohol undermine their effectiveness as leaders. Unfortunately, alcohol is often a contributing factor in many of the other issues addressed in this chapter, including fraternization, sexual harassment, and sexual assault.

Work/Life Balance

Factors such as geographic stability, career flexibility, and parenthood support can have a significant influence on many service members' decision to remain on active duty. The Navy has implemented a variety of new policy initiatives to retain its best officers and Sailors. Some examples of those initiatives include co-location support for dual-military families, increased maternity and paternity leave periods, and the Career Intermission Program, which allows eligible Sailors and officers to leave active duty for up to three years to pursue educational or personal goals. More information about these policies can be found on the Navy Personnel Command website at http://www.public.navy.mil/bupers-npc/support/21st_Century_Sailor/tflw/Pages/default.aspx.

Pregnancy and Parenthood

While starting a family is a personal decision, as a naval service member you are expected to balance the demands of a naval career with your family plans and responsibilities. The challenges that parenthood and military service present are not unique to one gender. Single parents, domestically separated parents, dual-military parents, parents who have custody of a minor child, and divorced service members with minor children are required to maintain a Family Care Plan (FCP). Because we must be ready to deploy at a moment's notice, the FCP is an essential document that obligates service members to establish and document plans to care for dependents in their absence. DoD Instruction 1342.19 series and OPNAVINST 1740.4D provide more information about the family care policy.

Timing of pregnancy for servicewomen can be a sensitive topic. The Navy encourages servicewomen to plan pregnancies to coincide with their shore duty assignment in order to prevent gapped billets in deployable units. This also helps prevent potential disruption to the service member's career and reduces any operational impact that would occur if a pregnant crewmember departed unexpectedly. Even young officers who do not plan to start a family immediately should be familiar with the pregnancy and parenthood instruction (see OPNAVINST 6000.1C), maternity and paternity leave policies (see MILPERSMAN 1050-430), childcare options, family care policy (see OPNAVINST 1740.4D), and other resources available. You may find yourself helping your Sailors navigate parenthood and military service while not being a parent yourself. You can also find more information on the Navy Personnel Command website.

Voting Assistance

The U.S. Navy voting assistance program is in place to ensure that eligible naval personnel have an opportunity to vote in federal, state, and local elections. Your command's voting assistance officer can provide all the materials necessary to register to vote for all elections. The key goal is to give every Sailor the opportunity to vote; it is not a mandatory voting program and should, of course, remain apolitical in its execution and approach. A good voting assistance program will reinforce commitment to our democratic principles and encourage every citizen's individual responsibility to participate in government.

Volunteer Programs and Charitable Causes

The Navy recognizes the importance of encouraging Sailors to engage with their communities both at home and while deployed. Every command should have a volunteer programs coordinator who plans and organizes community relations (COMREL) projects. These projects can be simple Saturday morning events such as cleanups at local beaches or larger and more far-reaching efforts such as building a playground for disadvantaged schoolchildren during a foreign port visit. Large commands in your area and embassy staffs in foreign countries can help you find great opportunities to make a difference in the community if you join your command's volunteer program.

Another way to get involved in your community is to support charitable causes. The Combined Federal Campaign (CFC) is a federal government–wide program that provides a listing of thousands of legitimate and reputable charitable causes and enables federal employees to make donations through regular deductions from their paychecks. CFC conducts a fund drive every year, and each command has a coordinator who ensures that everyone has the opportunity to support the cause of his or her choice. Additionally, the Navy–Marine Corps Relief Society, an organization dedicated to supporting our Sailors and their families in need, holds an annual fund drive separate from the CFC.

Understanding Our Values, Taking Care of Our Sailors, Accomplishing the Mission

The U.S. Navy focuses on "mission first, and Sailors always." From instilling our fundamental values to supporting Navy families and enhancing the physical, mental, and professional well-being of every Sailor, the Navy has programs and policies to support that mission. As a new officer you must strive to be aware of the programs and policies so you can support your command—and your Sailors—to the very best of your abilities.

8

Naval Correspondence and Administration

Although leadership at sea remains at *the* core of our profession, consider administrative management a core competency as well. As a newly commissioned officer, many of your first responsibilities will likely be administrative, and the importance of good administration will only increase over the course of your career, both for yourself and for those you work with. Administrative requirements intersect every aspect of naval life where mission accomplishment and results matter most, including mission, safety, personnel, and finance.

One way to build your reputation early at your first command is by demonstrating care and attentiveness to detail in the paperwork you handle. Ultimately, every product you approve or sign is a reflection of your standards. Treating administrative duties as merely "administrivia" (i.e., with only passing interest and minimal effort) is a sure way to jeopardize your command and your career.

If an officer neglects administrative duties, Sailors also suffer. Reenlistment forms, command awards, evaluations, recommendations, applications, and hazardous duty pay documents are just some of the types of paperwork that deeply affect your Sailors. Their quality of life and professional advancement will often depend on the documentation you submit on their behalf.

At both the individual and organizational levels, administrative management is a central component of time management. Identifying process efficiencies and learning to prioritize requirements will become increasingly valuable skills. Time is an invaluable commodity, and administration can result in savings or waste, depending on how judiciously you handle administrative tasks.

Your immediate boss will count on you to submit paperwork that is both clear and correct. Your chain of command will depend on you to anticipate deadlines, follow the references, and properly handle sensitive and classified information. Mistakes can be costly. Make sure that you have thorough knowledge of your administrative responsibilities and of every document that you put forward.

Strive for "All but the Signature" Staff Work

As you work on the myriad administrative requirements that a newly commissioned officer faces, think of yourself as part of a command-wide effort to improve performance and effectiveness. Your goal should be for your boss to approve every document you prepare without any amendments. Avoid the temptation of counting on someone else in the routing process to complete the package or fix mistakes. Your boss's experience may lead him or her to make changes or adjustments; use that as an opportunity to better understand the boss's expectations and preferences.

As you drive toward the goal of finished staff work, remember to ensure that your input is indeed complete. If an administrative package requires a cover memo or endorsement from your chain of command, for example, draft one for inclusion. As you are encouraged to do elsewhere in this book, ask yourself, "What would I want if I were the boss?" and you will be well on your way to meeting the "all but the signature" standard.

Anticipation and Planning

Life is busy at any naval command, and primary mission accomplishment demands thoughtful anticipation and careful planning in all areas, including administrative management. Your leadership responsibilities will encompass administrative deadlines as well as operational ones. Although the importance of timely paperwork and correspondence seems obvious, it bears emphasis because most junior officers (and senior ones, for that matter) will have to work very hard to meet deadlines, making those who manage these tasks effectively all the more valuable to the command.

Fortunately, you can plan ahead for the majority of the administrative work tasks you will face. Evaluations, end-of-tour awards, and end-of-year items such as command histories are all regularly scheduled requirements. Most successful commands maintain an "admin tickler" to track these deadlines; you should apply this concept to your own administrative requirements by maintaining your own admin tickler and cataloging all the scheduled reports, evaluations, and products that you will be expected to generate. By managing these well, you will be better prepared for the pop-up requirements that you can expect in the fast-paced environment you will live in as a newly commissioned officer.

Write Clearly

The writing style you use in a military setting will be different from the style you used in an academic environment. Naval writing shares many qualities with news writing; it should be more journalistic than academic. It should be clear, concise, and to the point. Keep it simple. Minimize the use of adverbs and adjectives. Focus on the facts, get to the main point quickly, and complete the tasking in no more than a page or two. As officers become more senior and face larger numbers of increasingly complex issues, their demand for precise, succinct writing only increases.

You can find numerous books and resources on improving your writing, so this brief section will highlight a few other tips. Avoid using all but the most commonly understood acronyms; superiors will quickly become frustrated by "alphabet soup." It's a good practice to use the full term first followed by the acronym in parentheses—for example, Aegis Training and Readiness Center (ATRC). Use the acronym thereafter to save space. Avoid using overly stiff language and the passive voice. Use plain language when possible, such as "Next time, we need to pay attention to current and wind," vice "Wind and current must be accounted for in the future and for all additional evolutions." Avoid using filler phrases unnecessary to the meaning of a sentence, such as "in the future" or "at this time."

Finally, make sure that you carefully proofread every document you submit, and make a habit of asking a peer to provide a second set of eyes for any work you drafted. Since most of your paperwork will be one or two pages long, try reading the document aloud to catch any missed mistakes and to check for ease of comprehension. Remember, your goal is not to have the reader marvel at your writing style but to help your seniors quickly assess the facts and make a decision.

Avoid Reinventing the Wheel

Most naval administration is repetitive (evaluations, supply orders, collateral duty designations, etc.), so locate previous examples to guide your efforts. Reviewing the last version—particularly a final, approved version that has been sent off the command—will demonstrate the established command standard.

In many cases, administrative requirements are so repetitive that your predecessor may have prepared templates to guide their preparation. No one will expect you to have these formats memorized, but you will be expected to review this information and know the latest version. If your predecessor did not turn over a file of common administrative products associated with your duties, you should build your own, both for yourself and for your eventual relief, and update it regularly. Check with your naval peers and your admin office for successful examples, formats, and templates.

What's the Reference?

Even when you have the previous example of an administrative requirement, you will want to review the reference that guides the program or product you are working on. If this is the first time you are responsible for the document, your boss will almost certainly ask you if you have reviewed the reference. No individual or command is perfect, so it is worth ensuring that the example your predecessor used is correct. Finally, naval references are routinely updated and streamlined, so a quick review will ensure that you are not using an out-of-date instruction. Your admin officer will have a catalog of all naval instructions for your use, but you should build your own quick-reference library (both digital and hard copy) for your most common administrative tasks.

The Point Paper

The U.S. Navy *Correspondence Manual* provides excellent guidance on writing naval memos and letters, but one of the most common products you will be required to produce is a point paper. This is usually a one-page memo that highlights a given issue, outlines several options to address it, and makes a recommendation.

Not all aspects of administration happen in an office. An ensign gives a safety brief prior to a crash-and-salvage drill.
U.S. Navy, MCSN Seaman Patrick Semales

If you bring up a dilemma or new challenge to your boss, he or she may ask you to "work up a point paper on the issue." Over time, if you encounter an issue or challenge you can help solve, you may on your own initiative compose a point paper to present your recommendations. The point paper can be a powerful weapon in your administrative arsenal. Be sure to ask for an example of a point or issue paper at your new command because each organization follows a slightly different format.

E-Mail Etiquette

Just as e-mail has impacted business and society in general, it has also permeated much of naval life. E-mail communications are now a staple of naval business and communications, and e-mail has enabled naval personnel to communicate much more easily both within and outside the lifelines of their commands.

Your comfort with e-mail in your personal and academic life, however, should not lull you into a false sense of complacency when it comes to e-mail in the Navy workplace. As you have likely discovered, e-mail can be forwarded quite easily, much more so than phone conversations or hard-copy communications, and an ill-considered comment in e-mail can quickly speed through the information superhighway. Once you click "send," your e-mail is extremely difficult to retract or erase.

Despite the potential pitfalls, e-mail is a necessary skill in the Navy, and it can save you work and time if used appropriately. If you are sending e-mail to a superior, address your senior by name ("Commander Jones") or at the very least "Sir" or "Ma'am," and finish with the appropriate closing ("Very respectfully" or "V/r"). Remembering these tips will keep you from having an otherwise solid e-mail not get the reception it deserves.

If an idea is overly complex or takes more than a few lines of text to explain, consider another communication format. A written memo, naval message, phone call, or face-to-face conversation may be a more effective way to convey your ideas. Recognize that in most quarters of the Navy, e-mail is still not perceived to be a permanent or "official" written naval message. A general rule is to respond to whatever tasking you receive via the same forum—answer a naval message with a message, e-mail with e-mail, and so on.

It is always good practice to avoid transmitting any message in anger, regardless of the forum, but e-mail's immediacy can make you particularly susceptible to emotional missteps. You are expected to give honest feedback and assessments; nevertheless, recognize that your message can be forwarded to unintended audiences with unintended consequences. Once again, give some thought as to whether e-mail is the best forum for the message you want to convey.

It can be difficult to express tone and context in e-mail, so don't automatically assume that the message sent is the message received. Even messages written with the best of intentions can be misinterpreted. Sometimes this cannot be helped. Establish your character and protect your reputation so that even if someone misconstrues your communication, the command community can help provide that person with the right context and assure him or her of your meaning.

Be careful not to convey sensitive or classified information on unclassified e-mail systems. The proper handling of classified material is covered later in this chapter, but it is important to state here that because of the ease with which information can be transmitted and disseminated, you must ensure the information you send via e-mail is appropriately classified and on the appropriate network.

E-mail "business rules" will vary from command to command. In some commands, your boss may prefer a simple status update via e-mail, while in others your boss may expect a face-to-face update. Check with your peers or a more experienced junior officer to find out what works best.

Finally, if you have bad news to pass to your boss, do not take the easy way out by sending an e-mail to avoid a tough conversation. Being a naval officer requires fortitude, and part of the job requires that you deliver the bad news as well as the good. If you are compelled to deliver tough news via e-mail because of distance or other operational constraints, take responsibility for the problem, don't make excuses, and provide the way ahead to a solution.

Counseling, Discipline, and Performance

Some of the most common—and important—administrative work you will do will be related to the performance assessment of your Sailors. The instruction that governs the Navy's performance evaluation system (currently BUPERSINST 1610.10D CH-1) is the principal reference for performance assessment. Many officers print out the most recent version of this instruction to include with their quick references because writing fitness reports and evaluations are continual requirements in the Navy.

The instruction will tell you when performance evaluations and formal counseling are required and how they should be prepared. It is worth reviewing periodically. Successful commands will be tracking performance evaluation timelines, but you should know the required reporting periods, anticipate deadlines, and ensure that your inputs follow the guidelines for the type of report needed.

In addition to these formal requirements you may be compelled to develop counseling sheets for Sailors who are not meeting standards in performance, physical fitness, and so on. While most Sailors are superb professionals, you will occasionally encounter one who has fallen short in some aspect of professional development. Documenting these deficiencies is critical, so be sure to touch base with your command's senior enlisted adviser and your department head to determine what format you should use when administering written counseling. Generally, this type of counseling should document the problem, identify deficiencies, provide guidance, and include a future date when the individual's performance will be reappraised.

If one of your Sailors commits an alleged violation of the UCMJ, he or she may wind up standing before the Executive Officer Inquiry (XOI) or Captain's Mast for punishment. Your command's legal officer will be able to assist your Sailor with the case and answer any questions you may have. In time (and generally after other leadership steps have failed) you may be compelled to draft a report chit against one of your Sailors who has violated an article of the UCMJ. As in all cases in which the UCMJ may be involved, seek out the advice of your department head and your command's legal officer to ensure that you are executing your responsibilities appropriately.

While the topic of nonjudicial punishment (NJP) is an important one, we will not cover it in depth here. Recognize, however, that as your Sailors make their way through the administration of the system, you will be expected to support them and assist with their needs. This does not mean that you will be required to defend their conduct, but you will need to work with your legal officer to ensure that your Sailors are receiving the time and services they need.

In many of these proceedings, you as the division officer (and likely your chief as well) will be required to provide a brief assessment or overview of the service member's performance to the CO or XO. Be prepared to provide this assessment, and be ready to field questions related to previous actions you have taken, such as formal counseling. COs dislike disciplinary proceedings as much as you do, and most administer NJP as a last resort. As they administer punishment, they will be very interested in the leadership and professional climate in which the affected Sailor works. Making sure that you have your "i"s dotted and "t"s crossed will assist the CO in assessing the case and prevent you from being unprepared.

Personal and Command Awards

You will also play a role in preparing awards for your Sailors. If you do not come from a military background, it is difficult to overstate how important this recognition is to Sailors—even if they say otherwise. With bonuses and other incentives largely controlled on a broad Navy-wide basis, awards are among the primary vehicles naval leaders use to recognize and reward strong performance at the command level. Recognizing your Sailors is a satisfying experience, but managing and administering the awards process requires effort.

The practice of looking to references and locating successful examples to guide your administrative tasks pertains to awards generation and management as well. In this case you should seek out the awards manual for your chain of command. Most carrier and expeditionary strike groups, for example, have issued their own instructions. You should also consult the *Navy and Marine Corps Awards Manual* (SECNAVINST 1650.1H) and the *DoD Manual of Military Decorations and Awards—Campaign, Expeditionary, and Service Medals* (DoD Manual 1348.33, vol. 2).

Awards generally comprise three elements: the citation, an awards form, and a "narrative"—a longer justification that details achievements to demonstrate why the nominee deserves recognition. Try to follow the award through the staffing process, from your first draft to the awarding ceremony, and compare the final approved citation to the one you prepared so you can refine your writing.

Planning ahead and tracking input deadlines will help ensure that your Sailors receive the recognition they deserve. You may occasionally have the opportunity to write an "impact award" honoring a specific and unexpected act of excellence by one of your Sailors, but you can anticipate the majority of award submissions because most occur at the end of deployments, the end of the training cycle of an operational command, or the end of an individual service member's tour. In many cases, commands reward Sailors completing their tour with a personal medal, so be ready to dedicate a significant level of effort to personalizing the decoration for each Sailor and ensuring that the details of their performance are in order.

Lean forward in collecting information and generating first drafts of awards packages for your Sailors. Enterprising young officers have been able to create opportunities for recognition by having things prepared for their boss's inevitable question, "Who do we want to recognize for this event?" Just as you advocate for your Sailors, your peers will fight hard for their Sailors as well. Understand that you may not be able to award a medal to every person you deem deserving. If this is the case, look for other ways to recognize good performance, such as a letter of commendation or a letter of appreciation.

In addition to awards for your Sailors, you may also play a role in preparing year-end awards for your command. Most commands compete for the Battle Efficiency Award as well as the subordinate mission excellence awards related to maintenance, safety, and warfare effectiveness. These awards usually require commands to create narratives of their achievements and meet certain performance milestones. To be ready for this, consider keeping a list of achievements over the course of the year so you are not starting from scratch in the eleventh month of a twelve-month competitive cycle.

References

As you prepare to win the "admin battle," consider building a small professional library to help you in this endeavor. You will find a number of the items listed below in your command spaces, but you may want to consider purchasing some of them after you have had a chance to review a peer's copy. If you do not want to print out a paper copy of the naval references, consider downloading a digital copy. Always check for the most recent version of the reference.

- *Awards Manual*
- Dictionary, any recent and comprehensive version
- *Division Officer's Guide* by ADM James G. Stavridis, USN (Ret.), RADM Robert Girrier, USN (Ret.), CDR Jeffrey Heames, USN, and CDR Thomas Ogden, USN (Naval Institute Press, 2017)
- File of previously successful reports and administrative products
- Navy *Correspondence Manual*
- Navy performance evaluation instruction
- Recurring reports tickler

Working with Classified Material

One element of your profession that separates you from the vast majority of your civilian peers is that you will likely work with classified material. Classified material is any information that, if disclosed to unauthorized people, could jeopardize U.S. interests, institutions, foreign relations, or national security. Three classification levels exist:

- Top secret: information whose unauthorized disclosure reasonably could be expected to cause exceptionally grave damage to the national security
- Secret: information whose unauthorized disclosure reasonably could be expected to cause serious damage to the national security
- Confidential: information whose unauthorized disclosure reasonably could be expected to cause damage to the national security

Given the critical nature of classified information, there are very clear directives in place to guide its use. As long as you have access to classified material, you will receive periodic security awareness briefings. Each command will have a security officer who will arrange these briefs to remind you of your responsibilities and inform you of security changes. As a condition of continued access to this information, you have an obligation to report any changes in your personal status to your security officer. Some of these changes include:

- Attempts by unauthorized individuals to obtain classified or proprietary information
- Loss or possible compromise of classified information
- Major financial difficulties
- Violations of the law or arrests
- Alcoholism or treatment of alcoholism or illegal use of drugs
- Involvement in court or legal proceedings

If you are working with classified material, you are normally required to work in a secure area. During the workday, secure areas are protected with a combination of access control systems, security, and identification badges. After hours, locks, alarms, and motion detectors are activated to prevent unauthorized access.

Need to Know

When sharing classified information with coworkers, you must be sure that they have not only the appropriate clearances and access levels but also a clear "need to know." Establishing need to know is important in controlling classified material. To make this determination, holders of classified material should ask themselves, "Why does the other person need the information?" If you have doubts about the person's need to know, you should either politely deny the person access or state that you need to seek additional guidance before providing access. Contact your security officer for advice.

Discussing Classified Information

To discuss classified program information you must use a secure area that has been specifically accredited for the particular programs to which you have access. Common passageways, bathrooms, dining areas, gyms, garages, commercial airlines, vehicles, and so on are *not* approved areas for classified discussions. When discussing classified material, you may use only secure communications.

The proliferation of personal electronic devices has also affected how we maneuver in command spaces. In most commands, personal electronic devices (telephones, smart watches, etc.) either are not allowed in a space that is cleared for classified information or should be turned off there. It is always best to ask about storing these devices when you enter a new building, particularly if you know you are heading there to discuss classified topics.

Do Your Best in All Things

Administration management may not be a naval officer's most glamorous duty, but your effectiveness in executing administrative tasks will be critical to the success of your command and the livelihood of your Sailors. Your ability to effectively save time for your leadership and to write with clarity and precision will be highly valued. Anticipating deadlines and meeting the "all but the signature" standard will mark you as a professional. And being conscientious about handling classified information will help protect our national security interests. As officers, we must strive to do our best in all things, even tasks that sometimes feel repetitive or routine, and effective administrative management skills will serve you well throughout your naval career.

9

Managing Your Career

Although the Navy values teamwork above all, this is a competitive profession, and you will ultimately be measured against a large number of other highly competent officers when your record comes before a promotion or screening board. The Navy's personnel selection system is regarded as highly fair; nevertheless, for you to reach your next career milestone you must understand what the Navy requires of you. Do not make the mistake of blindly going about your career without a thorough understanding of career opportunities and what it takes to promote to higher levels. Many officers you will interact with have stayed in longer than they originally planned (even those who were once convinced they were leaving the profession at the end of their first service obligation), so it is important to understand your options to prevent unintentionally closing out opportunities you may be offered in the future.

Promotion and Screening Boards

The Navy Personnel Command (NPC), often referred to as BUPERS, the Bureau, or Millington (after its location in Millington, Tennessee), uses a board review process to competitively select the best and most qualified officers for promotion and to screen candidates for various career milestones such as eligibility for command at sea. Promotion boards are "statutory" in that Congress dictates the number of officers that can be selected to each grade. Screening boards (also known as administrative boards) are largely governed by the Navy and the service community itself and are focused on selecting officers for further responsibilities within their community such as department head or command. The relevant websites on these subjects are:

- NPC promotion board page: http://www.public.navy.mil/bupers-npc/boards/generalboardinfo/Pages/default.aspx
- NPC screening board page: http://www.public.navy.mil/bupers-npc/boards/generalboardinfo/preparing_boards/Pages/AdminScreenBoard.aspx

The Detailer

The detailer is your direct representative at NPC. He or she "details" officers into specific jobs, balancing desires with career requirements and the needs of the Navy. When you reach approximately nine months from your projected rotation date (PRD) from your current command, you will begin a dialog with the detailer that concludes with orders for your next tour. As a starting point, discuss with your detailer what jobs may be available around your transfer window.

When your career, personal, and naval needs align, the detailing process can be relatively easy. On occasion, however, you may have to do a job that is not at the top of your preferences list. If you are detailed to a job that is not your first choice, "bloom where you are planted"—your strong performance in a tough job will almost always be rewarded over the long run. As you work through this process, remember that the detailer is an officer from your own community who can be a valuable career counselor; he or she sees hundreds of records from your community.

Unrestricted and Restricted Lines

Unrestricted line officers (often referred to as URLs or line officers) form the leadership of the Navy and its three traditional warfare communities: surface, subsurface, and aviation. They operate and command surface ships, submarines, aircraft, and the majority of shore installations. There are a good number of subcommunities within the line category, including engineering duty officers and special duty officers in public affairs, foreign area, and oceanography. These officers are largely drawn from the three major line communities after earning their warfare designation via a lateral transfer selection board process.

Staff corps officers (otherwise known as restricted line officers) have more narrowly focused, yet no less vital, responsibilities in support of commanders and the line communities. Unlike special duty assignment line officers, staff corps officers are initially commissioned into their fields. Often these specialists, such as supply officers and medical service corps officers, will work largely within one of the primary warfare communities. Each staff corps has a unique insignia worn on the left collar in place of the normal rank insignia (line officers wear rank insignia on both collars).

Typical Career Paths

All officers follow different career paths to success, but it is possible to lay out what a notional career might look like for each officer community.

Surface Warfare Officer

Surface warfare officers (SWOs) operate, maintain, and "drive" surface warships that continuously operate around the world. As a SWO you can expect alternating assignments between sea duty on an operational warship and duty ashore on a staff, program office, or training facility. The typical SWO career path is laid out on the PERS-41 website: http://www.public.navy.mil/bupers-npc/officer/Detailing/surfacewarfare/Pages/default.aspx.

As a new SWO, you can expect to do two division officer tours at sea soon after commissioning. During your first tour you will pursue numerous qualifications, culminating in earning your surface warfare officer pin. Your first two tours will together total approximately four years. Individual tour lengths depend on which division officer sequencing plan (DOSP) you elect (some officers will "fleet up" to a different job on the same ship, for instance, while others will go to a second tour job that requires a significant amount of schooling en route). Note: As of early 2018, the division officer sequencing plan was under review, so as in all service communities included in this chapter, it is prudent to check community websites for the most current information on a given community career path.

Following your division officer tours, you will go ashore for roughly two to three years. Most officers obtain a postgraduate degree during this period either using one of the Navy's educational programs or on their own time while

As you progress in the Navy, strong operational performance will factor prominently in your selection for future leadership responsibilities.
U.S. Navy, MCSN Declan Barnes

at another shore billet. Following your shore tour and department head training in Newport, Rhode Island, you will serve as a department head responsible for a major functional area on your next ship (usually operations, engineering, or weapons). Normal command tours begin at roughly fifteen years of commissioned service (you will serve fifteen months as the XO, then fifteen months as the CO), although earlier command opportunities are available for exceptional officers. For more information on both the conventional and surface nuclear pipelines, visit the PERS-41 website: http://www.public.navy.mil/bupers-npc/officer/Detailing/surfacewarfare/Pages/default.aspx.

Aviation

Aviation career paths are deeply affected by the particular community (e.g., F-18 Hornet, SH-60R Seahawk) an officer is assigned to, but communities share some general traits. Student naval aviators (SNAs) initially report to Pensacola, Florida, for the beginning of up to two years of training. While in Pensacola,

SNAs undergo aviation preflight indoctrination (API) and primary flight training, then are selected for one of three paths: multiengine prop, helicopter, or tail-hook (carrier aircraft). Intermediate and advanced flight training follow at various locations around the United States.

Upon completion of advanced training, aviators are "winged" and report to one of the fleet replacement squadrons for training in a particular airframe. Fully qualified aviators are then assigned to an operational squadron for their first sea tour. This path is essentially the same for pilots and naval flight officers (NFOs), with the exception that NFOs receive advanced training in weapons system operation vice flying.

A shore tour can follow after three years in an operational squadron, often as a flight instructor or assigned to a staff. The next operational tour is normally a "disassociated" tour on an afloat staff or as ship's company on an aircraft carrier such as assistant navigator or the "shooter" operating the ship's catapults. Officers screened for department head usually leave their disassociated tour after two years for fleet replacement squadron retraining and a job as a squadron department head for roughly three years. Following a post–department head shore tour, screened officers report to a squadron as XO, then "fleet up" to be CO after approximately eighteen months. The PERS-43 website contains additional information: http://www.public.navy.mil/bupers-npc/officer/Detailing/aviation/Pages/default.aspx.

Submarine Officer

Submarine officers operate and maintain the Navy's nuclear submarines. All submarine officers are nuclear-power qualified, which involves well over a year of formal academic training before the first sea tour. If you are accepted into the nuclear pipeline, you will report to Naval Nuclear Power Training Command in Charleston, South Carolina, for twenty-four weeks of intensive classroom training. After graduating you will report to one of the prototype shore-based reactors for six months of further training. At the completion of the training pipeline, the next stop is ten weeks at the Submarine School in New London, Connecticut, for the Submarine Officer Basic Course (SOBC).

Division officers can expect to spend thirty-two months on their first boat, qualifying in submarines (earning their gold dolphins) and serving as engineer officer. Two years of shore duty follow the first sea tour, during which many officers will earn a master's degree. Officers next attend the seven-month Submarine Officer Advance Course in New London and then report to their next submarine as a department head for thirty-two months. Successive shore and sea tours include a twenty-month XO tour at the twelve-year point, with command occurring at the sixteen-year point. The submarine officer career path can be found at the PERS-42 submarine website: http://www.public.navy.mil/bupers-npc/officer/Detailing/submarinenuclear/Pages/default.aspx.

Special Warfare Officer

Special warfare officers constitute a very small but incredibly capable and revered portion of the Navy's officer inventory. Officers can join the community through initial accession commissioning or lateral transfer. These warriors have proven their worth throughout this century's conflicts in Iraq and Afghanistan, and more senior special warfare officers are now rising to senior command and flag ranks. The websites below include excellent resources for new or aspiring special warfare officers:

- NPC SPECWAR site: http://www.public.navy.bupers-npc/officer/detailing/specwar/pages/default.aspx
- Navy SEAL site: http://www.sealswcc.mil/

Explosive Ordnance Officer

Explosive ordnance officers (EODs) are highly trained operators who lead small teams in rendering ordnance safe. They conduct these dangerous missions on land and undersea, and across every range of military operation. The EOD cadre is small in comparison with some other URL communities, and officers join the community through initial accession commissioning or lateral transfer. Similar to special warfare, more senior officers are rising to multiple command and flag ranks. More information can be found at the NPC EOD website: http://www.public.navy.mil/bupers-npc/officer/Detailing/EOD/Pages/default.aspx.

Staff Duty Assignment Officers

These officers are specialists within the line community, selected by a lateral transfer/redesignation board (one notable exception is the intelligence community, which does accept some newly commissioned officers). The competitive semiannual transfer/redesignation board selects the best-qualified officers for each community after taking into consideration the needs of both the gaining community and the candidate's existing community. Each type of staff duty assignment is briefly discussed below.

Engineering Duty Officer/Aviation Engineering Duty Officer
Engineering duty officers (EDOs) are involved in the design, construction, and repair of ships, submarines, aircraft, and systems related to naval warfare. All EDOs start their careers as line officers. After obtaining operational experience, interested officers apply for conversion to EDO through the semiannual transfer/redesignation board. New SWOs and submarine officers with exceptional academic records may apply for the engineering duty (ED) option upon commissioning. If selected for the ED option, you will be transferred to the EDO community upon warfare qualification and completion of your first division officer tour. More information is available at the NPC EDO website: http://www.public.navy.mil/bupers-npc/officer/Detailing/rlstaffcorps/engineering/Pages/default.aspx.

Full-Time Support
Full-time support (FTS) officers are Reserve officers on active duty who perform duties in connection with organizing, administering, recruiting, and training Navy Reserve components. FTS officers provide support to the Navy Reserve in the areas of manpower management, administration, mobilization, logistics, financial management, and facilities management. The FTS community is filled through the semiannual transfer/redesignation board from virtually all other officer communities. The FTS Community Manager site includes additional information: http://www.public.navy.mil/bupers-npc/officer/Detailing/fulltimesupport/Pages/default2.aspx.

Human Resource Professional
Human resource (HR) officers fill the need for professional administrators in the Navy's complex personnel management system. HRs serve on fleet, joint, and naval headquarters staffs and within the Bureau of Naval Personnel. These officers enter their community through the lateral transfer/redesignation process

either at the O-2/3 level if they do not have significant HR experience, or at the O-4 level with significant HR experience. More information is available at http://www.public.navy.mil/bupers-npc/officer/Detailing/rlstaffcorps/HR/Pages/default.aspx.

Oceanography

Oceanography special duty assignment officers enter through the lateral transfer/redesignation path after earning a warfare qualification in one of the line communities. Oceanographers work within nine warfare directorates that support operational commanders, and many specialize in areas such as physical oceanography or meteorology. Oceanographers are assigned to one of the fleet meteorological centers, major staffs, or research and development organizations. The NPC oceanography site offers extensive information: http://www.public.navy.mil/bupers-npc/officer/Detailing/IWC/oceano/Pages/default2.aspx.

Information Professional, Information Warfare, and Intelligence Officers

Information professional officers (IPs), information warfare officers (IWs), and intelligence officers (IOs) enter either through the lateral transfer process or, less frequently, are commissioned directly into one of these communities from the Naval Academy, Officer Candidate School (OCS), or the Reserve Officers' Training Corps (ROTC).

IPs provide a cadre of experienced computer network and radio communications specialists to support the Navy's warfighting requirements. They serve at sea on ships, on major staffs, at naval telecommunications centers around the world, and on acquisition projects.

IWs manage electronic warfare, signals intelligence, and cryptological functions for the Navy and on joint assignments. They work on major and joint staffs, at sea on larger ships, at cryptologic resource centers, at one of the three joint intelligence centers, and on related acquisition programs.

IOs serve as analysts and interpreters providing intelligence support on staffs, large ships, aircraft squadrons, and special warfare groups and to the joint intelligence centers. The websites for these communities can be found at the BUPERS IP website: http://www.public.navy.mil/bupers-npc/officer/Detailing/IWC/Pages/default2.aspx.

Foreign Area Officer

Foreign area officer (FAO) is a relatively new field that has emerged in recognition of the need for officers with extensive experience in specific geographic regions. Officers selected for FAOs are assigned a geographic region based on skill sets and interest. They can expect language training, if needed, at the Defense Language Institute (DLI) and academic training at the Naval Postgraduate School (NPS). The final phase of FAO training involves one to six months of in-country immersion to hone language and cultural skills. FAOs serve on staffs of fleets, combatant commands, and defense agencies as well as in DoD military-diplomatic offices at U.S. embassies and diplomatic posts. All FAOs must be warfare qualified and enter through the lateral transfer process. The FAO page discusses the requirements and purpose of this new field: http://www.public.navy.mil/bupers-npc/officer/Detailing/FAO/Pages/default.aspx.

Public Affairs Officer

Public affairs officers (PAOs) serve throughout the Navy promoting our message and supporting naval command staffs. PAOs attend the Defense Information School (DINFOS) at Fort Meade, Maryland, prior to their first duty station. This ten-week course covers the principles of public information and community relations as well as DoD policies. PAOs serve with combat camera units, the Navy News organization, and on all major and joint staffs. The PAO page on the NPC site includes additional information: http://www.public.navy.mil/bupers-npc/officer/Detailing/rlstaffcorps/public_affairs/Pages/default.aspx.

Limited Duty Officer/Chief Warrant Officer

Limited duty officers (LDOs) and chief warrant officers (CWOs) are drawn from the enlisted force and are commissioned to act as technical managers and to provide deckplate leadership. LDOs and CWOs are commissioned with a designator that is closely aligned with their prior enlisted rate. Because each designator is so narrowly focused, each has a unique career path. Fortunately, each designator has a webpage that lies within its broad parent community (surface warfare, aviation, submarine, or special warfare). The LDO/CWO Officer Community Manager page has links to each community: http://public.navy.mil/bupers-npc/officer/communitymanagers/active/ldo_cwo/Pages/default.aspx.

Restricted Line Communities

Restricted line, or staff, communities function in support of the unrestricted line and the Navy as a whole. The explanations given here provide an entry point for further exploration of each of the staff corps communities.

Chaplain Corps

Chaplains initially go through six weeks of training at the U.S. Navy Chaplain School in Newport, Rhode Island, and may attend several additional courses before being ordered to an operational ministry. A viable career in the Chaplain Corps will include a variety of tours—operational, overseas, hospital, and staff, and with the Coast Guard and the Marine Corps. Chaplain detailers advise career-minded chaplains not to stay in one geographical area for too long and—as with any other naval career—that taking the "hard" assignment counts. The U.S. Navy Chaplain website can provide more information on this service community: http://www.public.navy.mil/bupers-npc/officer/Detailing/rlstaff corps/chaplain/Pages/default.aspx.

Judge Advocate General Corps

U.S. Navy judge advocate generals (JAGs) practice criminal prosecution and defense, provide legal assistance to U.S. Navy and Marine Corps members, and assist naval commands. The JAG Corps is manned through direct accession as well as with officers from the unrestricted line who were selected for legal training. Direct appointment officers must be graduates of a law school accredited by the American Bar Association and must be admitted to practice by either federal court or the highest court of a state. Officer candidates attend a six-week indoctrination course at the Officer Development School in Newport, Rhode Island, followed by Naval Justice School. A great deal of information can be found on the Navy JAG website: http://www.jag.navy.mil.

Medical/Dental Communities

Navy medicine includes the Medical Corps, Dental Corps, Medical Service Corps, and Nurse Corps. Each is staffed through direct accessions and through in-service procurement programs from the enlisted and officer ranks of the Navy. Direct commission officers may be inducted at an advanced rank, depending on education and experience. New officers attend the five-week Officer

Development School in Newport, Rhode Island. Consult the Navy Bureau of Medicine site for more information on the great variety of subspecialties in the Navy's medical community: http://med.navy.mil/.

Supply Corps Officer

The Supply Corps constitutes one of the largest staff communities in the Navy. Supply officers serve on ships and submarines and in aviation units around the world. Supply officers generally specialize in a primary warfare community (surface, subsurface, or air) and further subspecialize in a particular field such as acquisition or fuels management. New officers attend the Navy Supply Corps School in Newport, Rhode Island, for roughly six months. Initial training includes the supply officer basic course, division officer leadership, and community specialization. The Supply Corps School maintains an excellent website that has a wealth of information: https://www.netc.navy.mil/centers/css/nscs/Home.htm.

Following initial training, you will report to an operational unit to serve as a division officer. Here you will likely earn your warfare specialty, such as the surface warfare supply corps officer (SWSCO) pin. The first operational tour is often followed by a tour at a shore facility such as one of the major Fleet Industrial Supply Centers (FISCs). Many officers will earn an advanced degree during their first shore tour, then go on to a second operational tour as a department head. Senior-level tours include management of major programs, sea tours on large ships such as aircraft carriers, and command of one of the many supply activities around the world. The NPC PERS-44 Supply Corps page is http://www.public.navy.mil/bupers-npc/officer/Detailing/rlstaffcorps/supply/Pages/default.aspx. Of particular interest is "It's Your Career," a PDF file in the Career Counselor section.

Civil Engineer Corps

Civil Engineer Corps (CEC) officers serve on major staffs and manage large construction projects around the world. They are uniformed professional architects and engineers who work in contracting, public works, and construction and run the Navy's construction battalions. CEC officers enter through ROTC, OCS, or lateral transfer. Newly commissioned CEC officers attend the basic course at the Civil Engineer Corps Officer School (CECOS) in Port Hueneme,

California, a thirteen-week course that comprises eight weeks of CEC orientation and five weeks of basic government contracting principles. All career-oriented CEC officers attend graduate school somewhere between their fourth and tenth year of service. The NPC CEC website includes more information: http://www.public.navy.mil/bupers-npc/officer/Detailing/rlstaffcorps/cec/Pages/default.aspx.

Career Management

All organizations have an embedded culture that values certain attributes and experiences in their employees, and the Navy is no different in that regard. Certain highly talented individuals will do well anywhere, but for most of us, an understanding of what the Navy expects from us goes a long way toward ensuring career success. This section introduces some of those expectations. The first (and always foremost) criterion is "sustained superior performance."

Sustained Superior Performance

Performance in demanding operational assignments is the basic currency of promotion and career milestone screening. For most officer communities, this translates into a frequently heard phrase: "sustained superior performance at sea." At every stage of your career, your CO will document your performance in an annual fitness report. Once you reach the rank of lieutenant, you will be competitively evaluated against your peers at your command (for LDOs and CWOs this competitive evaluation begins immediately). A note of caution: while breaking out ahead of your peers will be favorable to your career, teamwork and your willingness to help others are highly important as well; placing your own career above the good of the command or advancing at the expense of your peers is not the way to get ahead.

Community and Pentagon Tours

All officer communities will expect you to fulfill "community tours" in addition to your operational tours. These are the jobs that make the Navy and your specific service community run—jobs in major acquisition programs, personnel distribution jobs at NPC, or OPNAV tours (working on the staff supporting the CNO at the Pentagon). While these jobs may seem far away from your core operational profession, they are vital to the smooth operation of the Navy and are recognized as such by promotion and selection boards. For most officers, these assignments come after department head tours. Not all successful officers spend time in Washington, but your long-term career will likely benefit when you do (although excellence in the fleet remains the most important driver in your career).

Advanced Education

Most communities strongly encourage their officers to earn a master's degree. In some communities, a lack of advanced education may negatively affect your competitiveness as you reach command screening gates (check with your mentors to see how things work in your community). Fortunately, the Navy offers a wide range of advanced education options, including the Naval Postgraduate School in Monterey, California; the Naval War College in Newport, Rhode Island; and a wide variety of full-time overseas scholarship and off-duty options. Most degrees will lead to you being awarded a subspecialty code, which may determine what jobs you will be detailed to in the future. The Bureau's Education and Training Placement page provides additional information on educational opportunities for officers: http://www.public.navy.mil/bupers-npc/officer/Detailing/educationplacement/Pages/default.aspx.

Joint Professional Military Education

Joint professional military education (JPME) is required for all military officers, regardless of branch of service. The 1986 Goldwater-Nichols Defense Reorganization Act levied this requirement to enhance joint (i.e., multiservice) warfighting capability. You must complete JPME phase 1 prior to your command screening board; JPME phase 2 is required later in your career. JPME phase 1 consists of three courses (strategy and war, joint maritime operations, and theater security decision making) that on average take about one year to complete and can be earned via correspondence course or in residence at a war college. The NPC Joint Officer page has more information: http://www.public.navy.mil/bupers-npc/officer/Detailing/jointofficer/Pages/JPME.aspx.

Managing Your Record

In a very real sense, what your service record says on paper (or more accurately these days, onscreen) *is* you. Your promotion prospects, future assignments, and screening for major milestones such as command at sea are all determined by what is in your service record. Your service record resides at the NPC. The Navy does a good job of maintaining your record, but only you can make sure that it truly reflects all of the good things you have done in your career.

Pay particular attention to your officer data card (ODC) and your performance summary record (PSR). These online records are available only through the BUPERS Online (BOL) portal with a password or common access card (CAC). The ODC includes your officer service record (OSR), which lists all past duty assignments, education, personal data, subspecialty codes, and qualifications. The PSR lists all of your fitness reports. It provides the date, command, grades, and the reporting senior's trait average, which allows you to compare your performance against other officers your boss has evaluated.

The BOL site also allows you to order a CD that contains your official military personnel file (OMPF)—your complete service record. Savvy officers order their OMPF once per year to check that all documents are accounted for. There is also a handy board preparation checklist included that covers most service-record maintenance issues. Additionally, it is a good practice to keep a copy of all of your FITREPs, qualifications, and awards as a good backup that you can routinely reference. Some COs use your OMPF as a tool to mentor and guide you toward follow-on assignments that will help enrich your experience and ensure your competitiveness for future selection boards.

Your FITREP

You will receive a fitness report annually, the month determined by your current rank, as well as each time your reporting senior changes command. When you receive your FITREP it is important that you carefully review all of the administrative data for accuracy. Additionally, ensure that the dates your FITREP covers show complete continuity from your previous FITREP. This is vital for promotion boards to track day-for-day where you have been.

You will be evaluated on a set number of traits that will make up your trait average. As you review your FITREP ask your reporting senior what his or her "reporting senior's cumulative average" is. It is important that your promotion recommendations are increasing and your individual trait average is increasing against your reporting senior's cumulative average as your FITREPs progress. It is *imperative* that you ask your reporting senior any questions you have about your FITREP and performance prior to signing your FITREP.

Switching Communities

Most officers in support communities come from the three main line communities through the lateral transfer/redesignation board, which meets twice per year. Officers choose to apply for redesignation for a number of reasons, including interest, family concerns, and better career potential in a different field. This process is competitive, and each board selects the best-qualified officers for each community, taking into account the needs of both the gaining community and the candidate's existing community. Options for redesignation include the following:

- Aerospace engineering duty officer
- Civil Engineer Corps
- Engineering duty officer
- Foreign area officer
- Full-time support
- Human resources professional
- Information professional
- Information warfare
- Intelligence
- Medical Service Corps
- Oceanography
- Public affairs

There is also the opportunity to transfer between line communities (for instance, a few officers from other communities are selected for pilot training each year) or to one of the staff corps communities, such as supply. Refer to the BUPERS Lateral Transfer/Redesignation page for more information: http://www.public.navy.mil/bupers-npc/boards/administrative/TransferRedesignation/Pages/default.aspx.

Conclusion

Nothing can take the place of solid advice from your CO, other mentors, and your detailer, but the principles presented here are universal: sustained superior performance in operational billets and the effective management of the expected requirements of your respective service community are essential building blocks to a successful naval career.

Recommended References

- Bureau of Naval Personnel website: http://www.public.navy.mil/bupers-npc/Pages/default.aspx, the Navy's online source for career information.
- *Career Compass* by James A. Winnefeld (Naval Institute Press, 2005), an outstanding book of advice for the career-minded military officer.

10

Advice for Navy Spouses

Welcome to the Navy! Although it is your spouse or future spouse who is entering the Navy, you are joining the Navy family as well, and there is no doubt that you are also entering a new and exciting world.

Being a member of a Navy family holds incredible promise for travel, interesting places to live, and camaraderie. It also brings the challenges of absence and the adjustment to a lifestyle that will be different from civilian life. Simply put, military spouses also sacrifice and serve, and it is not surprising that the first person most military service members credit for their success is their spouse.

The goal of this chapter is to provide the spouse of the newly commissioned officer a short introduction to life in the Navy. For a more comprehensive view of marriage and family life in the Navy, consider the *Navy Spouse's Guide* by Laura Hall Stavridis (Naval Institute Press, 2002), an excellent book that provides far more detailed and broader advice for those who are married to members of the U.S. Navy. *Homefront Club: The Hardheaded Woman's Guide to Raising a Military Family* by Jacey Eckart (Naval Institute Press, 2005) is another helpful book that offers "married-but-single parents" practical advice laced with humor to address the unique challenges military spouses face.

Evolving Roles

While many spouses of past generations found life in the Navy family a rich and satisfying experience, most lived within a fairly rigid and formal social hierarchy and were expected to take on numerous social duties. In fact, spouses often received mention in an officer's fitness reports well into the 1980s! The advent of the two-career family and a general loosening in formality have made the life of a Navy spouse much less formal, if no less demanding.

Today's Navy recognizes that spouses, particularly the spouses of more junior naval personnel, often have careers of their own. As society has evolved to adjust to both spouses working outside the home, so has the Navy. Many officers, including COs and XOs, have spouses with their own careers, and you will also encounter naval peers who are geographic bachelors whose families live in another town.

Spouses now have far more latitude regarding whether and how much to participate in social interactions with other Navy spouses. Those who do will share a common experience, likely have more fun, and will have resources and networks they can rely on when they face the inevitable challenges military family life can bring. Spouses who choose not to participate may find their experience less collaborative and enjoyable; like most things in life, having good friends to share challenges often makes the experience more positive.

While the words and titles that are unique to the military may at first seem confusing and intimidating, just as in the civilian world, respect, consideration, and humility go a long way. Because the Navy is such a mobile profession and absence is a part of our lives, you will find most naval groups and families very welcoming. We all understand what it is like to be the new person, and most military families go out of their way to help the newly arrived feel welcome.

Useful Terms

There are several books that feature large glossaries of naval terms, and we suggest you consult one; again, the *Navy Spouse's Guide* is particularly helpful. The terms listed below are among those you will hear most often.

Wardroom—Term used to describe the officers in a command; it stems from the space on ships where officers traditionally meet and dine.
Ready room—Term used to describe the officers in an aviation squadron, as well as the space on an aircraft carrier where the aviators conduct their flight briefs and normal everyday business while at sea.
Deployment—Period of time in which operational commands serve away from home.

Inspection/Assessment—An on-site visit to a command conducted by off-ship experts to evaluate a particular competency or mission area. In many cases, a command's ability to deploy depends on a successful assessment, so preparations before an inspection or assessment may require more work and time from your family's service member.

Duty—Period of time in which naval personnel are required to stay at a command (potentially overnight) to provide security or administrative support.

Exchange or *PX*—Department store on base that only military members and their family can patronize.

Commissary—Supermarket on base that only military and their family members can patronize.

Leave—All naval personnel are afforded thirty days of leave per year. Leave is requested formally though a leave request form, or "leave chit," although these forms are now electronically managed. In operational commands (ships, squadrons, submarines, special warfare commands), leave plans will need to be balanced against operational or deployment schedules.

Liberty—Off-duty time. When naval personnel are not deployed, liberty is granted at the end of the current workday until the commencement of the next workday.

Social Events

Regardless of how much time you plan to spend (or can spend) socializing with your Navy family, some events you may choose to participate in are described below.

Hail and Farewell

The Hail and Farewell has few equivalents in civilian life, since employees in most civilian professions tend to move less frequently. Generally intended for the wardroom and its spouses only, the event's main purpose is to hail, or welcome, new members and their spouses and bid farewell to those leaving. Other than those broad outlines, however, the atmosphere can be as varied as the types of commands in the Navy. A Hail and Farewell can range from a roast of the person departing to a standard cocktail party.

As in any event related to gathering with coworkers, moderation in consuming food and alcohol is always a sound strategy, and you should never feel compelled to consume alcohol if you prefer not to. In many Hail and Farewells, spouses are also recognized and other spouses may be asked to say a few words. As a newer spouse or significant other, you will have few formal responsibilities other than having a nice time and getting to know some of your spouse's new coworkers and their husbands and wives.

Wetting Down

One of the most enjoyable customs in the Navy is the wetting down. Naval lore suggests that recently promoted officers should dedicate their first paycheck to celebrating their advancement with their shipmates in a gathering known as wetting down. Today's realities of family and finances usually make these celebrations more humble affairs, with junior officers often teaming up to host a combined wetting down. Although these events may be limited to officers only, spouses are often invited as well.

Social Outings for Spouses

Particularly during deployments or extended absences, the Family Readiness Group, a volunteer organization of spouses at a given command, may host events as varied as Halloween parties for the command's children and Halfway Deployment celebration nights. On a less formal scale, the spouses of commissioned officers may also choose to get together for a low-key dinner or event. Once again, these events are in no way mandatory, but participating will build relationships that will help sustain you during the times while your spouse or significant other is away.

Military Celebrations

Once or twice a year you will have the opportunity to attend a Navy Birthday Ball and perhaps a ball for your spouse's military community as well. These events are not inexpensive to attend, but they are usually priced to be a bit more affordable for junior members of the community and are most enjoyable when a large group of friends and shipmates goes together. If it is within your budget, consider staying at the hotel where the event is being held. Discounted rooms are often available, and making this decision both extends the experience and protects you and your spouse from driving home if you have consumed alcohol (although there is no pressure to consume alcoholic beverages at today's naval events).

RSVPs

Just as in your civilian social life, you will receive invitations for events that the host is hoping you will attend and is counting on your consideration to indicate whether you will accept or decline the invitation. Food, service, and a number of other details can hang in the balance while the host attempts to calculate the number of guests. Be considerate and do not inconvenience a prospective host by not responding to an invitation.

Leadership Roles to Understand

Commanding Officer

The commanding officer, often referred to as the CO, captain, or in some communities skipper (ask your spouse what is customary at his or her command), is the leader of your husband's or wife's command. The CO carries a responsibility and accountability that in many ways run profoundly deeper than that of a civilian CEO. At sea, COs carry particularly significant responsibilities for every aspect of their command's well-being and combat performance, but whether your spouse's first command is at sea or ashore, these leaders warrant your courtesy and respect.

When you are introduced to your spouse's commanding officer, it is perfectly fine to respond, "Pleased to meet you, Commander Jones," and then move on to general conversation. If you are not in the military yourself, the CO might invite you to refer to him or her by first name; if that is the case, feel free to do so. While the commanding officer will be deeply interested in how your spouse is adjusting to his or her chosen career, remember that the CO's amount of contact with your spouse may vary depending on the size of the command. In addition, depending on the size and style of event, the commanding officer will likely want to talk with a number of people, so once you have a chance to exchange pleasantries and engage in a brief conversation, be respectful of the CO's time and the other guests at the event who may be interested in communicating with him or her as well.

Commanding Officer's Spouse

Although spousal roles have evolved over the years, there is no mistaking that the CO's spouse still plays a significant leadership role in the command family and its social interactions. This role will vary greatly according to many circumstances (the spouse's profession, whether the spouse is co-located, the spouse's personal style and preferences, and so on), but she or he will be an important part of your Navy family.

Executive Officer

The executive officer, or XO, the second most senior officer at a command, will be in charge of the administrative and training needs of your spouse's command. Depending on the division of labor at the command (and the desires of the CO), the XO may be very heavily involved in the development of junior officers. If the CO is unmarried or a geographic bachelor, the XO's spouse may be the recognized leader in the wardroom community as well.

Command Master Chief

The command master chief (CMC) is the third member of the command triad. Charged with the care and development of all enlisted Sailors in the command, the CMC plays a prominent role in the command and is an excellent source of knowledge and experience. If your spouse is assigned responsibility for enlisted Sailors as a division officer, for example, the CMC will likely figure prominently in any quality-of-life issues the enlisted Sailors face.

Command Master Chief's Spouse

Like the CO's spouse, the husband or wife of the CMC is also generally viewed as holding a position of leadership among the community of families at a given command. Once again, this role will vary based on numerous factors, but the vast majority of these spouses are superb sources of experience and advice in their own right.

Department Head

While middle managers are often humorously maligned in popular culture, they are vital to well-run organizations, and the Navy is no exception. In most operational naval organizations, your spouse's first line manager will be the department head. While the relationships between the spouses of naval officers are far less formal and hierarchal, you will often find the department head's spouse to be another valuable source of help and advice.

Ombudsman

The ombudsman, appointed by the CO, is the official conduit between the command and the families. These very important leaders are vital to a healthy command and family community climate and are critical connections both for families looking for general information and for those facing specific challenges. If your command is one that deploys, the ombudsman will often maintain a phone message system known as the Care Line that informs families of a deployed command's status and news.

Family and Financial Matters

You will find that the Navy offers a great deal of help and information when it comes to your family and finances.

Pay

Just as you likely experienced when you viewed your first civilian paycheck, you will see a number of entries and deductions related to your partner's pay on his or her first naval paycheck (see chapter 6 for a more thorough discussion of the Navy's pay system). The vast majority of the military's pay system can be accessed through the program MyPay. Much of the information on MyPay is protected by passwords, and your spouse's permission is required for you to access his or her pay information. If your military member deploys or is away for an extended period, you may need a power of attorney to make broader financial decisions and actions (your spouse's command can help your spouse and you arrange this).

Family Emergency Planning

When a natural or manmade disaster strikes, you and your family should have a crisis plan already in place. The government site www.ready.gov provides exceptionally good advice for personal and family readiness planning. The *Navy Spouse's Guide* includes a complete description of the papers and material you should be able to access on short notice. The Navy also has a robust tool known as Ready Navy that helps service members and their families plan for emergency response during national emergencies and disasters. See https://ready.navy.mil.

Dependent Identification Cards

Your military dependent identification card is crucial to your ability to access military support. You will need it to enter a naval base, use the commissary and exchange, and enjoy the many other amenities on a base such as the gyms, MWR facilities, and so on. Safeguarding this card is critical, and replacing lost ID cards can be difficult (particularly when the naval member is away from home port), so treat this card with a care that equals or exceeds the care you take in handling your credit cards and driver's license.

The subject of dependent ID cards points to another topic that has frustrated many *future* spouses of military officers. Given the considerable access and financial benefits that these ID cards provide, and because of security considerations, fiancées are not issued military ID cards. This can prove logistically challenging for someone who no doubt plays an important role in his or her future spouse's life, but you should anticipate and plan for this.

Moving

Moving is a constant in the military profession (and in many other competitive leadership fields in the civilian world), and the Navy has made great strides in making the moving process more transparent and easier to plan. For a thorough description on the process, visit the website www.move.mil. Remember that to arrange a move in the Navy, you will need a copy of your spouse's military orders, the document that directs your spouse to transfer from one military assignment to another.

Despite the fact that the planning process has become a bit more streamlined, moves are still major family undertakings that generally occur every two to three years in a military family's life. Planning ahead and good communication among the military member, the military spouse, and the command are essential to keep the stress related to this process at a minimum. Many experienced military families have binders and files where they collect all the required information and receipts; you should seek out their advice as well as that of the Household Goods Office at your closest naval installation.

Visiting Your Loved One's Ship/Command

Just as there are appropriate times for your service member to visit you at your workplace, there are appropriate times to visit your naval member's command. Most commands will have clear visiting policies during the day and during the weekends. It is best to check the policy and avoid dropping by without notice. Operational commands can be inherently busy and sometimes dangerous to someone unfamiliar with the environment, so there are good reasons for these limitations. Additionally, just like your workplace, ships and commands are focused on getting the job done during the day.

Family Days

Some of the great memories of military family life stem from occasions when military commands share their activities with family members. Usually once a year or so, depending on operational schedules, your service member's command will invite families to visit their ship or command for the Navy's version of an open house. For surface ships, this may even include a short cruise. These can be very memorable days, and attendance is highly encouraged, but planning, preparation, and abiding by the command policies are essential to providing the best experience for your family. Occasions such as these are often less frequent in commands that are more shore based or administrative in nature, but family picnics and command events such as holiday parties will also be available for most military family members to enjoy.

Staying Connected

Your ability to communicate with your newly commissioned officer varies with his or her military assignment. Ensigns in many training commands do not have direct phone lines, and the most you will be able to do is leave a message. If you are one of the lucky spouses to have a military member who has his or her own desk and phone, remember to use it judiciously because recently commissioned officers have a busy workload day in and day out. Even though most adults today have a personal cell phone, the nature of your military spouse's work may preclude its use during work hours.

E-mail is often the most reliable way to convey routine information to a military family member, and most will have an opportunity to review their e-mail several times per day. You should not be alarmed or disappointed, however, if your loved one does not answer your e-mails immediately—particularly if the person is in an operational or deployed status. You may be initially frustrated that the Navy's lifestyle does not align with a nine-to-five desk job, but you will soon develop a communication rhythm with your spouse. Be mindful that security concerns prohibit disclosing official movement of a command via normal means, including e-mail.

Communications capabilities have rapidly evolved in the Navy, and fortunately, the days of military families communicating solely by posted letter every two weeks are long gone. Even when your loved ones are overseas or under way, they will be able to receive e-mail most of the time. In some cases, phone calls will also be possible at sea, but recognize that voice communications are a much rarer commodity at sea, so do not expect many calls. If you do receive a phone call, expect it to be fairly short because there will likely be other Sailors waiting to call their families as well. When your deployed spouse has the chance for liberty overseas, however, opportunities for phone calls are much more plentiful. Consider purchasing international calling cards or familiarizing yourself with an audio/video application on your mobile phone or computer before your spouse deploys. Finally, remember that even when phone calls are possible, your newly commissioned officer will likely be constrained in his or her ability to share certain details related to schedule and operations when a given command is operational or deployed.

Separations and Reunions

Long absences from your loved one are never easy, and deployments and other highly demanding periods are a fact of life for the newly commissioned officer and his or her family. The Navy Fleet Center and Family Support Centers, which are located in most fleet areas of concentrations, are wonderful resources for families dealing with separation; representatives from these centers often visit with returning military family members on their transits home following a deployment.

The challenge of separation when a loved one is on deployment is obvious, but reunions can pose their own challenges. Just as the military member has likely changed a bit on deployment, you and your family may have changed as well. The spouse who has remained at home has likely become used to making more decisions unilaterally, and children may now be used to dealing with just one parental authority figure. Successfully reincorporating a second adult figure into a household following a six-to-nine-month absence is a process that requires hard work, communication, and the understanding that everyone in the family will require some time to adjust and grow.

Expectations regarding what will occur during a returning officer's first day home are often the first point at which your respective visions can diverge if you are not communicating. The military member returning from deployment might want to spend a quiet day with family at home, while the military spouse, having singly managed the house, the family, and often a professional career as well, may be anxious to celebrate and reunite outside the confines of the home. With most postdeployment periods affording Navy personnel a week or two of leave, a good plan and good communication should enable both partners to meet their desires and expectations.

For more than two hundred years, homecomings have been special for the U.S. Navy and our families.
U.S. Navy, MC3 Joshua Rodriguez

Challenges and Rewards

Married and family life in the Navy offer many challenges and rewards. Although the challenges of separation, changing schedules, and the potential of your spouse going into harm's way all exist, you and your family will also have incredible experiences that include travel, living in many exciting areas throughout the country and the world, and the camaraderie of other great families who have chosen to support their loved ones' calling to serve their nation. Navy spouses and families also serve and sacrifice, but the rewards and satisfaction that await those who do are often extraordinary. If both partners remember to remain flexible and thoughtful, their efforts will help to smooth all transitions—moving, deploying, separating, and reuniting.

11

Basic Naval Management

Regardless of what community you join, things will get moving pretty quickly, particularly if you are immediately reporting to an assignment that involves management responsibilities. Even if your first tour as an officer is in a training command, many of the management tips in this chapter will be relevant when you do take on your first job in the fleet.

Initially you may wonder what your job is, what resources are available to you, and what special activities, training, and missions you are responsible for. Fortunately, there will be other people at your command who have done your job (or a very similar one) before you. Additionally, just as in other elements of life in the Navy, there are references that will guide you regarding the requirements and procedures related to your job. So whether you are starting your first job on a deployment or during a maintenance period, managing a well-run division or one that needs some work—you are not alone as you begin this challenge.

Turnover

Turnover, the process of one individual turning over a responsibility to another, is a concept that permeates many aspects of naval leadership and life. In a tactical situation, Sailors of all ranks conduct a turnover with their predecessors before assuming a watch position. A good turnover is equally important when one leader takes over responsibility for an organization (whether it is a squad, work center, division, or command) from another.

Commanding officers and flag officers often dedicate a week or more to conducting a turnover before taking charge of the commands they will lead. Similarly, whether you are a traditional division officer at sea or in a more administrative position, you will likely spend a few days with the person whose management responsibilities you will inherit. Young officers turning over for the first time will find a lot of information presented and not a lot of time to process it—the managerial equivalent of "drinking from a fire hose."

The person you relieve should be able to give you a good review of all the programs you will manage, the material condition of all spaces and equipment you will be responsible for, and your part in any upcoming assessments or missions that your command will undertake. It is imperative that you ask questions and take notes. Polite, detailed questions are appropriate, but be respectful of the experience and effort of the person turning over to you—do not be critical or identify things you plan to change. Your purpose is to gain an overall understanding of the organization you are going to lead and manage.

Questions to Ask

It is highly likely that you will be given a turnover notebook or briefing, but there are a few basic questions to have in your hip pocket. If you do not understand a term or acronym, ask the person to stop and explain—every person in the Navy was new once, and they will understand your lack of familiarity with certain terms. If it is not possible to ask the person right away, write it down to ask later. Examples of good questions to ask include:

- What spaces/buildings/equipment are you responsible for? (Make sure to visit every room or space in the organization you are responsible for during the turnover.)
- What programs are you responsible for?
- How are the divisional/squad/unit responsibilities divided up?
- Are there any ongoing personnel issues you should be aware of?
- Who are your primary points of contact for each area you are responsible for (internal to your command as well as external)?
- What publications and instructions are applicable to your area(s) of responsibility? Which ones have been most helpful to you?
- What unit- or ship-level instructions are you responsible for?

- Are there any collateral duties related to the primary job that you will be responsible for?
- What schools or enlisted manning are required for this division or unit? Are there any current or projected shortfalls?
- What training or exercises are required? How do you track them?
- What events in the next three to six months in the command schedule is our organization responsible for? How are preparations for those events coming?

Taking Notes

You will not be able to retain everything that is passed on to you by sheer memory, so keep a notebook with you at all times. As you process the information you write down, jot down additional questions as you think of them. Even after you are done turning over, keep your notes; you will find yourself referring to them well after the turnover process, and when it comes time for you to turn over your duties to the next young officer in a year or two, they will be a superb tool as you prepare for transferring these duties.

As you go through this process, the person you are relieving should show you where things are. The publications and instructions that outline the requirements for your job should be easily accessible. Remember, there is a reference for almost every managerial challenge in the Navy—even how to inspect a space or office. There should be copies of the command's instructions for you to review as well as information on required maintenance, personnel status, and documentation of all ongoing maintenance. You will probably not have time to review these references during turnover, but you will want to get familiar with them shortly thereafter.

Completing the Turnover

While it is not always required, you may have to route a turnover letter (see figure 11-1). Any significant issues—whether in the material status of gear you will now be responsible for or personnel issues that will affect your organization—should be in this letter. Once the CO signs that letter, you're it!

In some commands, turnover concludes very simply with you reporting to your immediate boss (often your department head), while in other environments you may be expected to personally report to a more senior officer to notify him or her that you have assumed the duties. If this is the case, ask your predecessor or other officers what is expected—the CO or XO may ask you a few questions to assess your knowledge of your new organization.

Talk with your chief and leading petty officers as well as your department head before completing the turnover process to ensure you have covered all the necessary information. Your predecessor may have informed you well, but he or she will soon depart, so be sure to also interface with the enlisted personnel you will be working with over the long term since they will be your teammates over the tenure of your first job.

Figure 11-1
Sample Correspondence

---

10 Jun 18

```
From:  ENS Sara J. Green, USNR, 123-45-6789/1110
To:    Commanding Officer, USS FASTSHIP
Via:   (1) ENS Joshua M. Smith, USN, 456-78-9123/1110
       (2) Engineering Officer, USS FASTSHIP
       (3) Executive Officer, USS FASTSHIP

Subj:  REPORT OF RELIEF AS ELECTRICAL OFFICER

Ref:        (a) OPNAVINST 3120.32D, NAVY SORM
            (b) FASTSHIPINST 3120.1A, FASTSHIP SORM
```

1. As of this date, I have officially relieved ENS Joshua Smith of all duties as Electrical Officer in USS FASTSHIP.

2. ENS Smith and I have jointly reviewed the records and programs under the cognizance of the Electrical Officer, as described in references (a) and (b). The status of those items is as follows:

    a) <u>Condition of all electrical equipment</u>. I have assessed the condition of all equipment under the Electrical Officer's cognizance and I find it in satisfactory condition with the exceptions noted in Engineering Department's Eight O'clock Reports.

    b) <u>Supervision and training of watchstanders</u>. All critical watch stations under the cognizant control of the Electrical Officer are adequately manned, trained, and supervised.

    c) <u>Material condition and cleanliness</u>. A walk-through of all spaces was conducted. Condition and cleanliness of all EE Division spaces is satisfactory with the exception of the electrical grade matting in the Tool Issue Room.

3. I accept all duties and responsibilities as Electrical Officer.

Sara J. Green

```
                                            Sara J. Green
                                            ENS      USN
```

Managing Your Division

With the fast pace of operational tasking and the need for your command to be surge ready, once the person you have relieved has departed, you will likely find yourself very busy keeping up with all the requirements and assignments coming your way. The personal qualifications you will be required to start working on and any collateral jobs or duties you may be assigned will compound the challenge.

Your division will be responsible for many items. If you attempt to tend to each item directly you will quickly become overwhelmed. Your chief and your leading petty officer will help you delegate and respond to tasking, and traditionally they assign individual responsibilities and tasks to the Sailors in your division. As a junior officer, part of your job is to help bring a broader perspective to your division members as you lead them.

Starting the Day

In most commands, ashore or afloat, you will be required to attend some sort of morning meeting. In commands where you have leadership responsibilities, you will likely attend a meeting for officers and chiefs followed by a meeting with your Sailors. In many commands, this initial morning meeting for all officers and chiefs is called officers' call or khaki call.

Whether the XO or another high-ranking officer runs this meeting, he or she will provide information about future events, outstanding requirements, and a laundry list of other information. Depending on how your command is organized, you may next find yourself at another short meeting at which the department head goes over his or her task list. The daily guidance you receive from your XO and department head will help you maintain the big picture, and it will be your job to keep your division members informed and ensure they will be ready to support the ship for future events. Remember to write down tasking! Not only are you looking out for the ship, you are taking care of your people by identifying and prioritizing their tasks.

Divisional Leadership Positions

Within your division, there will be people assigned to take care of different divisional responsibilities. Some examples include:

- Leading chief petty officer (LCPO)—the leading chief in your division and your main leadership partner
- Leading petty officer (LPO)—your senior petty officer, usually a first class petty officer
- Work center supervisor (WCS)—a mid-tier petty officer, usually an E-5, charged with leading one of your division's work centers
- Maintenance personnel—the remainder of your Sailors, who perform the maintenance on the systems and equipment associated with your division

Just as you will likely be assigned collateral duties, so will your personnel have many divisional-level collateral duties. While these duties are divisional in nature, they are also command-wide programs, so your Sailor who fills a

Not all management in the Navy involves paperwork. Here an ensign relays information during a training exercise.
U.S. Navy, PHAN Lamel J. Hinton

collateral duty will likely be receiving guidance from the command's program manager. These jobs may include safety petty officer; training petty officer; morale, welfare, and recreation representative; and electrical safety petty officer. You should make sure that your Sailors are fulfilling their collateral duties. If you take the view that any collateral duty someone in your division or unit holds is in many ways your duty as well, you will take a big step in ensuring the success of your division and your personnel.

Growing on the Job

The longer you hold a position, the more sure-footed you will become regarding your responsibilities. For now, your focus should be on learning the basics of your divisional responsibilities and building a relationship with your LCPO. These items should go hand in hand because your LCPO will play a significant role in training you how to manage a division. While individual strengths and weaknesses will dictate the nature of this relationship, one of the keys to success is to go to your chief first.

Be firm, fair, and consistent with your personnel. Hold them accountable, but be sure to praise in public and correct in private—unless there is a pressing and immediate need such as safety or preventing grave damage to equipment. Lastly, give credit where credit is due—if you have been complimented for something your division has done, be sure to relay those kind words to those most deserving—your Sailors.

Managing Programs

The term "program" refers to any set of requirements that must be managed and monitored to make sure those requirements are being enforced and maintained. Programs range from ammunition administration to electrical safety and cover everything in between. Many primary jobs have programs associated with their duties that will naturally fall to you; others will be unrelated to your primary billet and given to you as a collateral duty.

Getting Started

A good way to start managing your program is to review previous assessments that have been conducted, usually by following a checklist from the Navy instruction that governs your program. By analyzing the previous assessment—particularly if it was conducted by someone other than your predecessor, such as an outside inspector or subject matter expert—you will be able to focus on the areas of the program that warrant improvement. If your predecessor related these shortcomings and his or her efforts to correct them to you, this is a good sign that the program is "living and breathing." Conversely, if known shortcomings have not been addressed, this is also relevant information.

Some of the biggest building blocks of a program are the publications and instructions that govern it. Some instructions are updated more frequently than others. You will save yourself trouble by making sure your references are up-to-date.

Success is in the details. If one of your program's requirements is to make sure all equipment is properly bolted down, for example, you will want to make sure that all the right materials are being used for the job. Although you will not be the one bolting down the equipment, confirming that the proper bolts are being used and conducting spot checks to verify the proper installation will be among your responsibilities.

Documentation

If you are doing all the right things but can't show what you have accomplished, you are setting yourself and your organization up for failure. While most assessors are very experienced and will be able to tell if you are managing the program well, most also follow the philosophy that "if a requirement wasn't documented, it wasn't done." Having a well-organized binder to present your program to an off-ship assessor will not guarantee success, but documenting that you have consistently met the program requirements conveys a sense of follow-through that demonstrates you are meeting the objectives of the program.

Whether it is equipment logs, maintenance records, training reports, or counseling chits, let your shipmates know what documentation you require for your program. If you are not an organized person by nature, you will need to improve in this area because program management is a component of most leadership positions in the Navy. Ask your LCPO and LPO what has worked in the past and then work with them to implement it. You should also consider finding a few people on your ship who are known for good management abilities and take a look at how they organize and manage their programs.

Managing Assessments and Certifications

Assessments, traditionally referred to as inspections, are a fact of military life. Just as there is a requirement to pass Calculus I before signing up for Calculus II in college, your command will not be able to move forward without passing certain assessments and milestones. Not passing a course might delay graduation for a student, but failing an assessment could delay a ship, submarine, or squadron's deployment, and that might have Navy-wide repercussions.

Not every failed inspection risks delaying a deployment, but such setbacks affect morale and your ship's standing, and they often have ramifications on working hours and other quality-of-life issues. Most Sailors understand that mission comes first. More plainly, no matter how arduous, it is better to prepare well for an assessment once rather than having to prepare twice for the same assessment after falling short the first time.

Because of the importance of assessments and certifications, the time leading up to an assessment can be stressful. Part of your job will be ensuring that your Sailors understand the broader purpose of the inspection and the challenges ahead. If you believe that your Sailors will need to work longer hours than normal or during the weekend, first discuss this with your department head and chief, because many commands require that senior leaders such as the XO or the department head be aware that working hours have been extended.

In the best commands, each program and requirement gets the command-level attention and support it needs to be successful. Conflicting requirements, relative strengths and weaknesses of personnel, and the command's schedule, however, may not always allow this. As the manager of a given program, one of your roles is to be an advocate for your program, so be sure to convey effectively any training or command involvement required for the program's success.

As you prepare for the upcoming assessment, don't forget your other duties. There is a tendency to let non-inspection-related items fall by the wayside during the preparations for and execution of an assessment. Further, commands sometimes prepare for multiple assessments at the same time, which is to be expected in a Navy that prides itself on its ability to accomplish multiple missions at once. Through it all, remember to keep your head in the game and your standards high, and work hard in advance to avoid cramming for an assessment at the last minute.

Tactical Preparations

From the Supply Corps officer who tracks down and procures the parts necessary to keep a jet in the air to the antisubmarine warfare (ASW) officer who serves as the ASW evaluator when his or her ship is hunting a submarine, almost all junior officers have a tactical role to play. Tactical preparation starts long before any specific event. For aviators, for instance, this training starts at flight school. Each warfare community has warfare-specific publications and manuals as well as tactical memos and case studies. Make it a point to find out what is available, take the time to read the information you find, and—most important— practice the tactical skills and evolutions you will need to demonstrate.

Another way to maintain your situational awareness is to read message traffic, the Navy's system of transmitting plans and policy via radio broadcast. While quite a bit of message traffic is administrative in nature, most tactical information is transmitted via message traffic or via a classified website known as the collaboration at sea (CAS) site. If there is a training exercise coming up, there will likely be a preexercise message giving the specifics for the exercise.

If your CO is the officer conducting the exercise (OCE) or the officer in tactical command (OTC), you may in fact have to draft this message yourself. If your ship or command is taking part in an actual operation, there will be messages that come out in relation to that specific operation's goals and requirements. The daily intention messages (DIMs) and other warfare-area-specific messages will hold valuable information as well.

You may also be required to attend meetings and briefs that will reinforce what you may have already read and let you know of any recent changes to the planned exercise or operation. You may be required to draft or even deliver a portion of the brief—particularly if there is a tactical evolution associated with your division's principal duties.

If you are responsible for building a tactical brief, take this for the opportunity it is by finding briefing templates that work, using the current references, and practicing your brief ahead of time in front of your department head to identify any information gaps in your presentation. Even if you are not involved in giving a brief or required to attend briefs, it is a good idea to attend them if you are allowed to do so. You will likely learn quite a bit, and this will contribute significantly to your professional development.

Managing Up

One of the most important relationships you will have is with your immediate superior. There is an old saying that you can manage your boss or your boss will manage you. Rather than take this somewhat adversarial view, think about your working relationship with your boss as a constructive relationship in which you are the junior partner.

"Managing up" does not imply manipulating or placating your boss through a well-turned phrase. What it does mean is keeping your boss informed of what is going on in your division. If you do this well on a consistent basis, you will demonstrate a command of your organization's requirements that will make your boss much more comfortable with your approach and much less likely to micromanage your efforts.

Your department head will expect quite a bit from you. Expect him or her to ask many questions. You may not know all the answers at first, but you should make it a point to avoid failing to answer the same question twice. Be sure to write down what your boss asks for and to follow up appropriately if you do not initially have an answer ready.

While you are certainly entitled to ask for clarifying guidance, you should not expect your boss to provide all the details for the task at hand. That is your job. It's fine to ask about the due date or the format of the desired product (a written report, an e-mail, or a verbal confirmation, for example). If you think there might be a genuine obstacle to completing a task, find time to discuss that, but avoid the appearance that you are pushing back on a request or attempting to demonstrate how busy you are.

In the beginning, your boss will expect you to have questions. If the deadline permits, though, it is a good idea to do your own research before asking questions. Consider asking a fellow junior officer first. For something within the lifelines of your organization, ask your chief. If you still have questions after doing your homework, then ask your boss, but in a way that shows you have already done some research on the issue.

One of the key elements of managing up is leaving your boss room to maneuver should an unforeseen obstacle occur. The best way to do this is by completing your assignments early or on time. Determine your boss' strengths and weaknesses and be prepared to adjust to them. Focusing on what is best for your boss in relation to meeting a requirement will also help you tailor your methods for success. The bottom line is that when your boss succeeds, so do you.

Managing Collateral Duties

Collateral duties are a part of naval life that you will likely encounter shortly after arriving at your first command. Collateral duties you might be assigned include:

- Legal officer
- Morale, welfare, and recreation officer or MWR funds custodian
- Public affairs officer
- Voting assistance officer
- Wardroom mess treasurer

Depending on the collateral duty, you may find yourself reporting directly to the XO and CO or to another senior officer. You may feel intimidated because of their rank and position, but keep in mind that they will largely have the same needs as the leader to whom you normally report. Simply put, they will want to ensure that your management of a particular collateral duty is meeting the interests of the command.

If you are reporting directly to the CO or XO, it is a good practice to keep your immediate senior informed as well. Just as any collateral duties that your junior personnel own are also your collateral duties to a certain degree, the same goes for your boss. Even though your boss may not have a direct interest in your collateral duty, your time management directly affects a part of the organization's effectiveness. If you keep the boss in the loop, he or she will be able to work with you to balance your other demands; for example, when experts outside the command are assessing one of your programs.

Collateral duties can be rewarding. Helping a Sailor gain American citizenship or register to vote is a very satisfying experience. While your principal focus should always be on your primary duties and operational performance, tackling collateral duties in a positive and focused manner also demonstrates that you are ready for more responsibilities in the future.

Planning and Executing

Much of your planning and executing will simply be assessing what needs to be done and doing it, but two items can assist you with large-scale planning and evaluation: a plan of action and milestones (POA&M) and a checklist.

Plan of Action and Milestones

A POA&M is a delineation of all requirements related to a comprehensive project, with a timeline and responsibility assigned for each step. Frequently centered on an upcoming inspection, deployment, or another complex goal, this plan (often a Word or Excel document) provides a clear path to the end goal.

POA&Ms are well-used tools at most successful commands. When you begin preparing for a major milestone, locate a POA&M that your more experienced peers identify as particularly effective. You could use this same approach to prepare for significant challenges in your management portfolio as well. Usually broken down in blocks of time before the inspection or deployment (e.g., six months, three months, one month, one week), the POA&M breaks large goals down into more easily managed elements while leaving time to address issues as they come up.

Driving the Checklist

Checklists, also known as check sheets, are very prevalent in the Navy. They often provide step-by-step guidance for accomplishing a task within specifications. There are also checklists for program management as well as space inspections and divisional requirements (e.g., electrical equipment requirements). Just as you should make sure to use the most recent publication, make sure you are using the latest version of any check sheet because they are updated frequently.

Once you obtain the most up-to-date check sheets for your areas of responsibility, read through them yourself. Generally, references are listed at the beginning of the document or are related to each item on the check sheet. Check sheets often offer a "guided tour" through the instructions that dictate the specifics for your program, and it is worth your time to become very familiar with the items on your check sheets.

As you use these documents to evaluate where you stand, the most important thing is to be self-critical. If you are your own toughest critic, you can find discrepancies before the assessors do and fix problems beforehand. If a problem can't be fixed in the short term, it can be documented for a longer-term solution. Finally, when you are done using a check sheet to analyze a program or complete an evolution, add it to your files. These check sheets demonstrate consistent program management and will often pinpoint when a problem was identified or fixed.

Ensuring Quality

In a traditional naval division you may not physically be completing the work for which your division is responsible, but you play a significant role in ensuring the quality of your Sailors' work. Your LCPO will be your most valuable partner in this effort, particularly in terms of the technical aspects of your organization's responsibilities.

Administratively, you will be required to route a number of reports and documents through the chain of command. From leave chits to training reports, after your chief looks at the item in question, the chits will be forwarded to you for your review. When reviewing a document, read every single block where information is required. If it is a training report, make sure it is in the proper format, that all training requirements for the period of the report are met, and that the supporting documentation required (i.e., muster sheets and critiques) is attached and complete.

Spot Checks

The maintenance, material, and management system (3M) is integral to our operational fleet. If you have never worked with the system before, the initial terms may seem foreign, but 3M is a core program that ensures our Navy's capability. Preventive maintenance done correctly prevents unplanned equipment failure. Just as you change the oil in your car every three thousand miles or so to extend the life of your car, preventive maintenance on a ship focuses on conducting inspections and servicing and replacing parts with specific life spans to keep equipment operating longer.

As a newly commissioned officer, you will likely be required to do maintenance spot checks frequently as a quality check to ensure your personnel are following the guidelines for accomplishing maintenance. Questions to keep in mind as you conduct a spot check include:

- Is the person conducting this maintenance properly qualified to do so?
- Is the correct/most up-to-date procedure being followed?
- Are the correct tools, lubricants, and parts being used?
- Is the person following the procedure exactly?
- Does the person know what safety precautions are applicable to this procedure?

Division in the Spotlight

Your command's Division in the Spotlight (DITS), in some commands also referred to as the command excellence program, is another way to ensure quality across the board for the entire ship or command. While the method and name of this program may vary, most commands in the Navy have some variety of a comprehensive review of a division's or department's readiness. When it is your turn, your DITS inspection will likely include:

- A 3M spot check with the CO and/or XO
- Program reviews
- Uniform inspection
- Zone inspection of the spaces for which you are responsible

Program reviews will be completed by the command's program manager or resident subject matter expert. These reviews will likely be compiled into a single report, presented to the CO, that will create a portrait of the overall health of your division.

Some commands issue a schedule ahead of time to allow you to prepare for the review. Other commands conduct a more random selection to promote sustained readiness by not allowing divisions time to surge for an inspection, relax, and then surge again when the inspection occurs again. If your predecessor has copies of the last DITS, this will be a very effective tool to get a quick sense of the overall readiness of your division.

Challenges and Rewards Ahead

The wide variety of topics in this chapter points to the many responsibilities you will encounter in your first managerial job as a commissioned officer. Persistence and a positive, steadfast attitude will serve you well as you tackle these challenges. While many tasks will demand that you strive for perfection, sometimes it is better not to let "perfect" get in the way of "good." The art of "majoring on the major issues and minoring on the minors" is one that you will develop with time. Remember, you were commissioned because numerous people along the way decided that you have what it takes to be an officer in the world's most powerful Navy—you can do it!

12

Getting the Most out of Naval Schools

New ensigns almost invariably attend a naval school in support of their training pipeline to their first assignment. Whether you attend a more comprehensive school such as naval flight school or a shorter course such as the engagement control officer course for the Tomahawk weapon system, naval schools will play an important role in your professional development.

Although going to school may feel like a break from your primary professional duties at your command, you will want to give these schools your best. Naval schools are "free" knowledge in that they enable you to gain new skills or improve old ones without the strain of real-world operations or the downside of real-world mistakes that sometimes occur during on-the-job training in an operational setting. But in other ways, these courses are anything but free. The Navy is paying for this school, both in terms of the cost it takes to run the course and in terms of time that the course is taking you away from your principal duties.

Of course, there are other reasons to take these courses seriously. First, the instructors are often naval leaders who have been handpicked to share their expertise with you based on their own success in the fleet, and it is smart to heed their advice. Second, unlike some of the academic courses you have taken in the past, many of these courses are directly related to a core or collateral duty, so you will want to pay attention because you are likely to be asked to demonstrate what you have learned in a real-world setting. Third, more naval schools are reporting student performance to parent commands. Fourth, and most profoundly, your ship and your Sailors will be counting on you to bring back what you have learned to your command. This recurring theme that your performance affects not only you but also a much larger group of people is one that new naval officers will continually encounter.

Chain of Command

Naval schools adhere to a chain of command just as traditional duty stations do. Your instructors will report up their own chain of command to a department head, who in turn reports to the commander of the school. While the actual links in the chain of command will vary, it is important to remember that naval schools often take a much more holistic approach to student development than the standard civilian institution does.

Section Leader

In addition to the assigned staff, many schools customarily designate a member of the class to be the class or section leader, usually based on seniority. The class leader's job usually involves taking attendance and handling basic logistics

Figure 12-1
Helpful Hints: How Naval Schools Are Different from College

- Naval schools are a military commitment. Just like a muster on a ship, do not be late, and be prepared to participate in the same way you would be ready for duty or work.
- It will not be just you who will be affected by your performance.
- Unlike the college experience that you have largely left behind, naval schools help to build your service or business reputation.
- Sometimes you cannot take homework home. Because you may be working with classified material, your study may be restricted to certain areas in the naval school compound.
- Navy schools often require you to live in temporary lodging for a period of a week to a few months away from your normal place of residence.
- Because naval schools may feature activities involving more risk such as small-arms training and live firefighting, safety will be stressed much more heavily.

related to classroom administration. In some cases, the section leader will be the first person with whom you discuss any leave or liberty request. As you might imagine, peer leadership can sometimes be thankless, so do your best to be supportive and responsive to the section leader. Soon enough you may be a section leader for a naval school, and you will appreciate the same treatment from your classmates.

A section leader's responsibilities can be very broad, particularly for naval schools that have lengthier terms, so your section leaders will likely ask for volunteers to whom they can delegate portions of their responsibilities. These duties could include being a watchbill coordinator for classroom duties such as security, maintaining the coffee mess, or arranging a class event at graduation. While the lesser side of human nature might incline you to avoid pitching in, do your best to find an area where you can help. By pitching in you are doing the right thing, and in many cases these relationships with your school classmates will contribute to your fleet reputation over time.

Staff Mentors

In larger courses, a more senior officer and member of the staff may be assigned as your class leader or mentor. These officers (or senior enlisted leaders) are valuable resources both during the course and later in your career.

In some cases, staff mentors fulfill many of the duties that a section leader might otherwise fill, and student section leaders directly interface with the staff mentor. Once again, your best approach will be to comply promptly and positively with the staff mentor's direction and be a good teammate by pitching in on whatever project or task may be required to support the class. If these leaders are senior commissioned officers, you will also want to ensure that you are giving them the respect that their rank and position warrant; even though you may be sitting in the classroom, they deserve the same respect that you afford senior officers in the fleet.

Commanders of the Schools

Most schools, even those with short courses, are part of a broader array of courses that constitute a naval school command. If you are in a school with longer courses, the commander of the naval school command may visit your class. Just like the dean of a civilian college, these leaders have had successful careers—not in the field of academics but in the fleet. With this in mind, be respectful of these leaders if you encounter them, but also realize that in many schools students rarely interact with the commander of the school.

Instructors

Instructors are the lifeblood of naval schools. These subject matter experts will often be senior in rank to you, but some may be experienced senior and junior enlisted. While they will respect your rank, they will have positional authority over you in your class and are charged with your education and your safety, so give them the respect they deserve.

Learning Smarter, Not Harder

Most junior officers have previous academic experience and have learned how to follow basic studying fundamentals to succeed. If you are among a lucky few, your natural talent and intelligence may have allowed you to succeed in

Not all Navy schools take place in the classroom. Members of a BUD/S class participate in the intensive physical training that is one of the hallmarks of the SEAL community.
U.S. Navy, PH2 Eric Logsdon

previous academic environments without following an organized study regimen. In many naval schools, however, time will be short and the academic material may be new, so it is best to follow good academic practices. Even if you are confident, remember that your performance in your naval course will be important not just to you but also to the men and women who will be counting on you in the fleet.

Cooperate to Graduate
The Navy is in a real sense a team sport, and many of its schools reflect this spirit of teamwork and encourage collaboration through group projects and study groups. As always, make sure that you understand the policies regarding collaboration—as efficient as a group effort may be, you never want to sacrifice your integrity merely to improve your performance in a naval school. If the school's policies do allow for student cooperation (and keeping in mind that you will still have to take the exams yourself), you can often improve your learning by joining study groups.

Participate in an Outline Exchange
In longer classes, it can really help to have each class member compose an outline of a given lecture or assigned reading and share that with members of the study group or perhaps the whole class. Once again, ensure that this is legal, and do not skip reading the assigned material merely because you have someone else's outline; instead, use the outline to complement your own preparation. Keep outlines on hand because they can be very helpful when you are reviewing for a test. Beware of older outlines that have been passed down from previous editions of the course; information often changes as practices and procedures evolve in the Navy.

Read the Syllabus
Almost every naval course has a syllabus—a document that specifies who is teaching the course, what the readings will be, the topic, and other course-related requirements. Take some time to review the syllabus because it will help you to prepare for lessons and perhaps also allow you to identify the subject matter expert for a given area if you have problems. And be sure to retain it after you return to your duty post, both for review and to share with your peers.

Find Your Best Place to Study

The quality of your study time can be hugely dependent on where you study. Be realistic about your powers of concentration and your ability to avoid distractions and pick the place where you can most effectively and efficiently prepare.

Read the Assignment before Class

Some of the concepts in a naval course may be fairly specialized and new to you, so read the assigned course material before the instructor discusses it. This may seem like common sense, but many students in and out of the military make the mistake of counting on the instructor to teach them the material while they receive the information passively without preparing for the lesson. You will learn much more effectively by reading the material beforehand.

Go to the Review Sessions

The form and content of course material review sessions can vary, but generally the instructor will focus on the concepts he or she thinks are important, and these concepts will likely appear on the test. Review sessions often occur outside normal class time and are voluntary, but they are almost always worth attending. If this is a longer course with several tests scheduled, attending the first review will also give you a good sense of how reliable the reviews are for future tests.

Seek Out Extra Practice or Instruction If You Need It

While some naval courses are more theoretical, most are taught to equip you with a particular experience or skill. The faculty will certainly be interested in helping you to develop that skill, but you will often be the best judge of how you are progressing.

Just as in civilian life, some students will have a prior background or innate aptitude that allows them to pick up a specific skill more quickly than others. If you are not that type of person, look for additional opportunities to practice the skills the course is teaching you. Everyone wants to do well in front of his or her peers; just remember that making mistakes in the classroom—and learning from them—will allow you to move past those obstacles when you are expected to perform those duties in the fleet.

Getting the Most out of Naval Schools — 145

What If You Already Know the Subject Matter of the Course Well?
Because some naval courses are periodic requirements for every command in the Navy, you may wind up in a course that touches on a subject matter area where you already have a great deal of experience. If this is the case, be courteous to the instructor and your class by serving as a helpful asset in the class rather than showing everyone how smart you are.

The Navy is constantly reviewing its course subjects, so several things may have changed since you last took the course or were trained in an area. In the last decade, for example, there have been a number of changes to the main space fire doctrine (MSFD) that ships use to combat fires, changes a student who last concentrated on this area some time ago might not know.

If you are attending a naval course that covers familiar material, use this as a chance to enhance or reaffirm your knowledge. Even if the course is a complete repeat for you, remember that getting a chance to build "your muscle memory" in an activity your command is counting on you to master never hurts.

Preparing before the Course
Work with your command's school coordinators to find out what the prerequisites are for a given naval course. The prerequisites for some courses include physical, medical, and training requirements that will compel your command to have a whole program in place to ensure that you are eligible and prepared for the training. In reality, the prerequisites and requirements are usually not that extensive for most courses, but you will want to use a little advance planning to make sure that you are as prepared as possible.

If the course you are attending is fairly common, check with more experienced junior officers to see if they attended and if they have any material from the course. Talk to them about their experiences and explicitly ask them what they wish they had known about the course before starting it. Scanning or quickly reading any materials they have retained will give you a better sense of comfort as you begin the course of instruction. Finally, if you live in the same town where the school is located or arrive there a day or two early, make a dry run to the class location the day before class. This will reduce your stress on the first morning and prevent you from being late on the first day of class.

Being late to class on the first day of any school is never good, but in some naval courses you could lose your spot (more formally referred to as a "quota") in the class if you are late. Many naval courses are so sought after that commands will send potential students to the first day of class on "standby" in hopes of replacing a student who failed to show for class. In addition to being on time, make sure that you arrive in the correct uniform as well.

After the Course

Keep your notes if this is permitted. Although class notes will not substitute for reviewing the reference that guides a given subject area, your notes will give you a great ready reference of the material. Because most naval schools focus on a topic or skill set you will rely on to perform your job, you will find yourself returning to previous course material much more often than you likely did for courses in college. Remember that course material and lesson guides can become obsolete, so always ensure that you are reviewing up-to-date naval references.

If the course offers CDs or printed material, be sure to take those as well. This material will often play a role in a qualification board if it is related to the core competencies of your specific service community. Be a good shipmate and let your department head and peers know that you have this material to share. This will ensure that the next person from your command to take the course will also be well prepared. Finally, many naval school commands and instructors will provide contact information so that you can get in touch with them if you have a question after the course has ended. Being able to reach back to the instructors of a previous course can clarify a question that is critical to your command's performance during an inspection or an exercise in the fleet.

Other Considerations Unique to the Naval Classroom

Naval schools can be very different from traditional academic experiences, so there are other aspects of naval coursework to consider as well.

Administration

Every naval course you attend will require orders. These may be as simple as one-page no-cost orders to attend a school near your parent command or one of many intermediate stops included in a longer set of orders associated with a permanent change of duty station. You will need to ensure that the school's administrative staff endorses these orders. Your orders will likely be required to enable you to stay at a combined bachelor quarters (CBQ) near the school you are attending. If you are away from your permanent command, make sure that you retain your lodging receipts and travel receipts to support filing a travel claim to recoup your expenses after the course.

Security

Throughout your naval career you will be entrusted with sensitive material; the material at naval schools is no exception. Students in the Navy's more comprehensive tactical schools handle quite a bit of classified material so do not be surprised to see extra safeguards in place. For instance, you may have to periodically serve as the student who secures the classroom at the end of the academic day by ensuring that classified safes are locked. Naval schools have programs in place to inform their students what the classification of the course material is and how that material should be handled, but if you have any doubts, ask your instructor for guidance.

Course Critiques

The Navy prides itself on continually focusing on improvement, so you will almost always be asked to provide feedback on a given course. This should not be taken as an opportunity to settle old scores or take a free shot at a tough instructor. Make your feedback honest and constructive. No one likes to come up short in the eyes of a student, and most instructors want to best the best teachers possible in order to pass on their knowledge to students effectively. Concentrating on areas that you found particularly helpful as well as areas you wish were more comprehensively covered is usually a good approach. If you observe a shortcoming or behavior that is truly troubling early in the class, do not wait to share this information in the course critique at the end of the course—seek out your section leader or instructors right away.

Leave and Liberty

Since naval schools represent an investment in you and an opportunity cost in terms of others not attending, taking leave or liberty during normal workdays will be discouraged (holidays and winter breaks are the usual exceptions). If there is a compelling personal need that you believe may necessitate leave (the birth of a child, for example), discuss this with your section leader and staff mentor as soon as you sense this situation may emerge. As in the fleet, sharing your challenges with your school chain of command in a timely manner gives them the greatest opportunity to help you.

Standing Watch

If the course is particularly long or is housed at its own facility, you may be assigned some watches or required to stand duty for a day. Such responsibilities are usually small or infrequent, but perform them to the best of your ability. Once again, people appreciate a team player.

Beyond the Classroom

In addition to what you will learn in a naval school, there are a number of other considerations beyond the classroom to keep in mind in order to get the most out of these important educational opportunities.

Get to Know Your Classmates

Lifelong friendships have started in naval classrooms. As in any activity in life, it is best to have friends who can share common experiences, so look to connect with the students who share the classroom with you. Besides the human dimension, you will be surprised at how much you can learn from officers from other commands. Over time these relationships can prove helpful and can give you a perspective outside the lifelines of your command when you are looking for advice or merely want to know what it is like in another command in the Navy.

Get to Know Your Instructors

Although your instructors are placed at the head of a class to do a job, try to get to know them as well. If they are senior officers or enlisted leaders it would be inappropriate to pursue a peer relationship with them, but some instructors become lifelong mentors for their students. Additionally, most instructors have been detailed to their positions based on their career success and subject matter knowledge. While you will always want to be authentic and respect the faculty's time, making a small connection with them and staying in touch afterward might prove beneficial down the road if you have a question or issue after you leave the course.

Live Close to the School

If the school is a long one, choose a place to live that is nearby. While many training schools outside your home port will strongly encourage or require you to live in a CBQ, some longer schools will be classified as a permanent change of station, and you will be allowed to pick where you are going to live.

Living more than thirty minutes away from where the course is taught will affect your quality of life—particularly if you have to make two round trips daily to support night study. The vast majority of naval courses will commence and conclude during regular business hours—the heart of rush hour—so be sure to ask about rush hour commute times (better yet, test them yourself) before committing to an otherwise great place that is farther away from your school.

The longer the course, the more likely night study will be involved to prepare appropriately for the exams. If your course is tactically oriented, some of your course material will be classified, which will almost make it a certainty that you will have to return to the classroom at night to study.

Attending a Naval School in the Same Area as Your Command

If your school is short and in the area of your command, make it a practice to return to your command after school unless your boss tells you differently. This may not be feasible for some of the more demanding courses, but doing this will ease your burden when you complete your coursework and will signal to your chain of command that you have not lost sight of your core responsibilities.

Returning to your command at the end of a school day is not always easy, and many young officers have observed that schools outside their home port area tend to be easier to manage, but in the long run, returning to your command is a sound practice. A quick visit that allows you to briefly scan your naval e-mail accounts, touch base with your chief on the week ahead, and scan your in-box for any new assignments will help prevent you from feeling overwhelmed or badly surprised when you return after completing your school. Even if it is impossible to come back every day, periodically visiting your parent command will make things much easier for you when you return to your primary duties.

Watch Your Conduct

Although you may feel far away from your home command while you are attending a naval course, in some ways you have never been closer. When you are at school you are a representative of your command. Many commanding officers have received a complimentary phone call—or a negative one—that helped to establish a young officer's trajectory. So in addition to being a good steward for your command while you are in the classroom, be mindful of your conduct outside it.

As you should at all times, avoid alcohol-related misconduct, particularly driving while under the influence of alcohol. A DUI, or any other legal interaction with the police, will inevitably make its way back to your parent command. Simply put, make sure you are making responsible choices in both your academic and social lives.

Get a Workout and Get Your Sleep
Unlike the shared efforts and high-adrenaline deadlines that often keep your job vibrant during the day in your normal work environment, academic settings will usually demand that you have better rest. Most of us have struggled in the classroom with concentrating more on staying awake than on the course material at hand—do not let this happen to you.

Managing rest can be especially tricky for officers attending a course and returning to their command each night. Particularly if you are in a duty section, you may be asked to stand a watch when you return to your duty day following the school day. Although this will likely only happen every few days, do everything you can to work with your duty section leader to avoid going to school with only three to four hours of rest.

In addition to being well rested for your course, you should also keep up with physical conditioning. For a shorter class, this will help you stay alert in class. For longer courses, particularly those where you are living away from your parent command, you will want to stay fit and avoid returning to your command a few pounds heavier—an easy trap to fall into if you are eating out more frequently while you are away from home.

Have Fun
If you are attending a naval course outside your home port that lasts more than a week, look for some weekend activities beyond watching television in a hotel room or going to the closest bar. All naval bases have a morale, welfare, and recreation (MWR) representative who can help you identify attractions in the

area, sporting events, or even day trips that you would enjoy. Although there is certainly nothing wrong with grabbing a drink with friends or watching a ballgame on television, look to enhance your experiences as you progress through your career by more fully exploring the areas you are assigned to—one of the genuinely fun aspects of naval life.

Leading and Learning: A Way of Life

Naval schools are one of the great components of the Navy's commitment to lifelong learning while you serve. Few professions invest as heavily in continued education, and as a newly commissioned officer your commitment to these courses should be absolute. Your command, your shipmates, and your Sailors deserve nothing less, and the lessons you learn in the classroom may save lives in the fleet during times of trial.

13

Voices of Command

Although leadership abounds at all levels in a successful chain of command, no one sets the tone for the command more than the commanding officer. As you begin your first few months as an ensign, your interaction with your captain may range from daily interaction at a small operational command to much less frequent contact in some larger commands. Even the best COs may have demands on their time that preclude them from giving you direct advice and counsel on what a brand-new ensign can do to succeed. In this chapter, several distinguished commanding officers from a variety of service communities pass on their advice to you.

Time Management: The Universal Challenge

Before I move on to the subject at hand, I must first congratulate those of you who are reading this as you prepare to report to your first ship. What you have chosen to do is extraordinary; serving one's country is an act of great selflessness, and as a retired naval officer, I am grateful to every young man or woman who chooses to serve this great nation, especially in the U.S. Navy.

You are about to undertake a life quite unlike the one you left behind, irrespective of your commissioning source. For those of you joining the fleet from Annapolis, you will now take for granted time and freedom that were doled out to you previously as privileges. For those of you joining the fleet from NROTC, you will get used to a whole new level of structure and rigor in your once carefree lives. And for those of you joining your first wardroom from the enlisted ranks, you will be exposed to a far different professional atmosphere than the one you left on the mess decks or the CPO mess, one that places demands on you that you did not previously have.

The one thing that ties all of these experiences together is the absolute necessity to manage your own time. Nothing you have done thus far has prepared you for the incredible demands that will soon be placed on your time. Thrust out into the working world now with some money in your pocket to enjoy the finer things in life, you will arrive at the ship often before the sun rises and just as often leave after the sun sets. You will have to spend time learning how to be a good leader and manager (and you must be both), tracking down repairs and seeing to the development of your people, even as you are faced with a grueling and often relentless need to develop your own professional skills. You will have demands placed on your time by your friends, family, and spouse or significant other. Oh, and by the way, you will need to spend time tending to your own physical fitness to stay within standards.

What I am describing is a witch's brew of conditions that will make you believe that there are not enough hours in the day to do all the things you need to do. Without developing a solid set of skills and tools designed to manage your time effectively, you will quickly fall behind the power curve, a curve that some simply never transcend. To provide a bit of insight into what some of those tools might be, I humbly offer the following, and I hope one or more of these tools might be of use to you.

- Goals are for chumps; plans are for winners. Everyone has goals; winners actually achieve them. Achieving goals is a function of the dedicated application of time and energy to a set of preplanned milestones chronologically ordered in a manner designed to achieve the objective. Write down your plans. Share them with your boss; ask his or her opinion on how logical or achievable your plan is. Work with your chief to devise plans. Constantly update your plans. Don't make a plan and then set it on the shelf, and don't make a plan that you are unwilling to alter. Make your subordinates plan, and make them show you their plans. Effective planning is one of the most effective ways to conserve your most precious asset: your time.

The commanding officer not only leads his command tactically but is also the most senior mentor on the ship.
U.S. Navy, SN Jessica Pounds

- Guard your personal time jealously and use it effectively. The Navy expects you to maintain physical fitness standards, so carve out time to work out. During the course of the workday, carve out time in which you can work on your priorities without interruption. Of course, your boss or the CO or XO can interrupt, but tell your chief that you really need this time. Use it to plan, use it for your own professional

- development, use it to read and answer your e-mail. But be ruthless in protecting it, and that means protecting it from the newfound (and less-disciplined) friends you will meet in the wardroom.
- Make time to be social. One of the very best things about wardroom life is the social aspect, replicated almost nowhere else, and certainly not in the corporate world. Be open to social events with your shipmates. Hang out with each other, help each other navigate the world that each of you inhabits. Everything in moderation, including fun. Going to sea is too hard a life for there not to be a good bit of fun bound up in it. Enjoy it.
- Before you leave the ship each day, take the next day's plan of the day (POD) and use it to plan out your day, including personal time. Discuss this personal plan the next day with your divisional leaders so they know what your priorities are. It is much easier to get blown from one thing to another when you don't have a plan.

The emphasis I place on time management is not something I came by late in my career. I was lucky enough to have people early on tell me how important it would be, and by the time I was fortunate enough to command my own destroyer, I taught and mentored a generation of officers in how to be more effective. I wish each of you great good luck, and I urge you to quickly discover how best to manage your own time. It will make all the difference.

—**CDR Bryan McGrath, USN (Ret.)**, retired in 2008. He commanded USS *Bulkeley* (DDG 84) from 2004 to 2006, during which the ship earned the USS *Arizona* Memorial Trophy and the Battle Efficiency "E," and he earned the Surface Navy Association's Zumwalt Award for Inspirational Leadership.

Never Wait to Make a Difference

First and foremost—welcome to the Fleet!

You are embarking on an incredible journey. Along the way you will serve with some of the most dedicated men and women our great Nation has to offer, make friendships that will last a lifetime, and share experiences that will exceed your grandest expectations.

Your naval career will also afford an incomparable opportunity to make a difference at a relatively young age. If you think about your childhood friends who went into different career fields, few can boast to have the sheer responsibility and authority that you will at the beginning of your time in the fleet. You will be landing planes on aircraft carriers, conducting missions as Navy SEALs, navigating ships as surface warfare officers, or one of a multitude of other real-world missions where your hard work and dedication will have an immediate impact on the unit you are a part of. Equally as important, regardless of your specialty, is the opportunity to lead, mentor, and learn from the enlisted Sailors that you'll serve with.

Throughout my career I've been thrilled to work with a multitude of young officers who made an impact well beyond their pay grades. These are officers who not only performed their assigned duties as pilots, submariners, surface warfare officers, and more, but who invested a little extra effort to become the very best at what they do. In doing so they elevated their commands and propelled those they served with to new heights.

But what are the characteristics that set these officers apart from their peers? What enabled them to make such an outsized difference? Was it merely a function of hard work, dedication, and the relentless pursuit of excellence? To help you on your way, I'd like to offer up three recommendations for your consideration.

First and foremost, *become the master of your craft*. Almost everything you experience as a new junior officer in your first command will be new—the people, the mission, and the command itself. The sheer amount of information and opportunities will at times feel a bit overwhelming, and you're likely to be pulled in a lot of different directions. You'll have opportunities to grow and develop at work, spend social time with friends, and visit and explore local attractions . . . and you should make time to do each of these things and more.

To be true value-added to your unit, however, you'll have to *become the master of your craft*. This means seeking out and understanding everything there is to know about your profession and the specific role you play in your command. The finest officers I've had the pleasure of serving with are the ones who dedicate themselves to this purpose; quickly finding mentors who can help guide their path; read widely to immerse themselves in their profession; and share their lessons with other junior officers.

Second, *stay intellectually curious.* The Navy revolves around repetition. No matter your professional field, you're likely to be bound by checklists and routine, whether as part of a watch team or within your unit, and there's always the risk that after a year or so you will start to feel like you're living a scene out of the movie *Groundhog Day.* As you master your craft, use your familiarity with your job to start asking questions like "Why do we do it this way?" and "What's the history behind our current way of doing business?" Your intellectual curiosity will serve two purposes: it will keep you fully engaged in your current job while leading you to discover knowledge that will make you a treasured asset to your command.

Last, *claim ownership. Make* things happen, don't *let* them happen. All of us wearing a Navy uniform are really good at identifying the problems that exist with our jobs, in our units, and in the Navy. You'll find that you spend countless hours discussing with your friends the issues that you wish were better. The road less traveled is to take action after identifying areas for improvement, and you'll likely be surprised at just how easy it is to make positive change. I've worked with many a junior officer who recognized a shortcoming with a current procedure or way of doing business, determined why we did it that way, carefully weighed alternatives, then took action to make improvements. These officers are worth their weight in gold to any organization because they've claimed ownership of their unit, and their actions speak louder than words ever can.

As a commanding officer, I gave the keys to the kingdom to officers who mastered their craft, stayed intellectually curious, and claimed ownership for the command.

Let me leave you with a final thought and a recommended theme for your career: *Never wait to make a difference.* I've watched as many Sailors during my career—from junior enlisted to senior admirals—hesitated to act on great ideas. In some cases, they felt that they had to attain some arbitrarily higher rank before they would be in a position to implement the ideas or the changes they thought were needed. In other cases, they were simply afraid to fail.

Don't be seduced into choosing not to act *now* because it isn't necessarily the right time. You will be presented with opportunities to make a difference early in your career, and I encourage you to take them. As the saying goes, "fortune favors the bold." Be willing to take calculated risks throughout your career, and never wait to make a difference. You'll be pleasantly surprised by the outcome.

> —**CDR Guy Snodgrass** commanded Strike Fighter Squadron 195, a forward-deployed F/A-18E squadron homeported in Atsugi, Japan. Ashore, he served as special assistant to Secretary of Defense Jim Mattis, speechwriter to Chief of Naval Operations ADM Jonathan Greenert, and as a Top Gun instructor. A 1998 graduate of the U.S. Naval Academy, he holds master's degrees from the Massachusetts Institute of Technology and the U.S. Naval War College.

Managing Relationships, Maturity, Passion, and Trust

My first meetings with new officers at a SEAL team are in equal measure discussing my expectations of them and determining their strengths, weaknesses, interests, and special skills to slot them in a platoon or other job on the team. How does each person fit into the team beyond whatever billet is to be filled? Platoon officers often weigh personality matters quite heavily because the relationship between the two officers in a platoon, chief and LPO, goes a long way in making a platoon better or worse than the sum of its parts. In this vein, I ask a lot of questions about the reporting officer's background, education, unique personal experiences, language skills, and training experience. In the last instance, I also want to know with whom they went through training, both officer and enlisted, because it is sometimes necessary to break up classmates into different platoons.

Throughout this process of getting to know the new officer and mentally slotting him within the command, I discuss my expectations. I concentrate on three things. I start with what traditionally can be a real issue for new officers in the SEAL teams: trying to be one of the boys. New officers may have gone through training with them and know them quite well, but their relationships must now evolve. This can mean different things to different officers. Some understand and are already living the concept; others require additional counseling by the XO, platoon chief, or platoon commander. In rare cases, officers are at the opposite extreme and are too aloof. This problem is actually far more difficult to address, and it is one that a new officer usually does not outgrow with time at the command. This problem is rare, though, and there is a large range between overly aloof and overly familiar within which to develop a suitable leadership style. The majority of officers ultimately find their personal style; some just need to be guided and reminded of where it is.

I next focus on a broad area I label maturity. I discuss many things here, but it can be best summed up as understanding what the role of an officer in the SEAL teams is and realizing that it is much more than pure operational prowess. SEAL officers should be strong operators, but they also need to be strong leaders. Moral courage, personal responsibility, and self-discipline are all aspects of this leadership. The basic underwater demolition team/SEAL (BUD/S) mentality of "if you're not cheating, you're not trying" has to now be tempered with the realization that their actions can have serious consequences for themselves and others.

Finally, and tied closely to the notion of leadership, is passion. I want the members of my command to be passionate about what they are doing. They need to master the skills of the trade, not just learn them or be exposed to them. This is hard because there is a lot of ground to cover, but I ask them to be the best they can be and to supplement their training with professional reading. I believe that new officers should read not just about SEAL operations but also about a diverse range of subjects, because you never know what might turn out to be helpful. I also encourage them to work on their skills as communicators because—whether giving an operational brief or writing an evaluation—communication skills are essential to being a leader. These skills make for successful missions and get their personnel promoted and recognized.

Following this initial guidance I continue to assess these officers and watch how they develop through training and gaining experience. As our predeployment training nears its end, I begin to assess the most important thing of all: my combined rational and intuitive assessment that an officer has my full trust and confidence to lead SEALs and other assigned personnel in combat. This is more than just the sum of operational skill and leadership. The element of trust enters into it. I have had great leaders and operators, but without this trust and confidence, it is all for naught.

For me, trust is built on a continuing relationship with an officer where periodically I see that the leader does what is right in a variety of situations. He does not have to always do what is absolutely right but what he thinks is right at the time, given the information at hand. This is a lot higher bar than it seems, and not everyone can get over it. But as we prepared to deploy some platoons to Iraq, this trust in an officer's judgment and confidence in his skills was essential.

Given the opportunity to command again, I would stress that what I look for is an officer who continuously and passionately works to develop and refine his skills as a leader and operator while doing what is right given the information he has at the time.

—**RDML Alex Krongard, USN (Ret.)**, a graduate of Princeton University and the National War College, commanded SEAL Team 7 during a deployment in Iraq, for which he was awarded the Bronze Star.

Motivation, Intellect, and Example

> When a capable officer has the deck, the discipline and safety of the ship are intact. Conversely, when a deficient officer has the deck, discipline breaks down and safety is compromised; the ship might not run afoul, but its reliability will be that of a drifting wreck.
>
> —CDR Vincent D. McBeth, USN (Ret.)

Your service as a commissioned officer in a warship places you at the nexus of people and mission where responsibility peaks and accountability is absolute. The first precept of a division officer is to learn and understand the standing orders, battle orders, and commander's intent. Command of a warship is not a reward doled out to those in good favor or for time served; the privilege of command is recognition of professional mastery. A warship relies on the knowledge, experience, and judgment of its captain. The captain is responsible and accountable for the safety of the ship and the performance and discipline of the crew. As a division officer, you fill an important leadership role in the ship.

The operating environment of a warship at sea is chaotic. Your obligation is to ensure that the captain's knowledge, experience, and judgment as articulated through orders and intent bear on all situations. The captain expects you, as a leader, to act on your training, of your own initiative, in accordance with his or her intent and in compliance with the standing and battle orders. During an officer of the deck qualification board a young officer was asked, "Why should the captain qualify you as officer of the deck?" The young officer replied, "Because the captain cannot be on the bridge twenty-four hours a day. As the officer of the deck, I act by, with, and through the captain to serve as his eyes, ears, and voice." I doubt there is a more complete answer or expression of the trust, faith, and confidence demanded by a captain of the officer of the deck.

A warship is not judged by the awards it receives but by the performance of its crew in the preparation and execution of combat operations. Excellence in engineering, seamanship, navigation, communication, warfighting, and damage control, to name a few, represents the "Float—Move—Communicate—Fight" ethos that translates combat readiness into action. Training and disciplined execution ensure a warship's combat readiness and are fundamental to operational success and mission accomplishment. In my mind, and validated by my own experiences in command, if a warship lacks the fundamentals, nothing else will sustain it when challenged. As a division officer, you will be called upon to execute the tactics, techniques, and procedures outlined in the ship's doctrine. To do so effectively you must possess the discipline to act without prompting to accomplish assigned tasks. In short, combat readiness is the foundation for success in all shipboard operations, in peacetime and war, and disciplined execution is its hallmark.

The greatest asset of a warship is the talent, energy, and dedication of its Sailors—your shipmates. In this regard, the importance of your individual leadership cannot be overstated. There are tremendous reservoirs of untapped potential within each of your shipmates waiting to be tapped by a capable leader. As a leader, your task is to evoke the highest individual performance from each member of your team. Evoking high individual performance starts with setting the conditions for growth, learning, and teamwork. It requires you to identify the values the surface warfare community seeks to cultivate, nurture, and sustain from one generation to the next. Among these values are duty, honor, mission, and integrity. Remember, followers confer leadership. As a division officer, you will be given subordinates; as a leader, you will have to earn followers.

Your efforts will at times be greeted by disinterest and reluctance from seniors, peers, and subordinates. You must demand that your shipmates act boldly in action and deed, and insist on doing right without concern for personal consequences. The tools at your disposal are numerous. I recommend you start by focusing on three: motivation, intellect, and example. I value motivation in an officer more than any quality except judgment. Motivation will lead you early in your naval career to take charge of your own professional development. The power of your intellect will yield well-reasoned decisions that demonstrate sound judgment. Finally, the power of your example will focus the efforts of your division and guide each member to act in a manner that will always honor those for whom we serve—country, shipmates, family, and self.

As Aristotle explains, "We are what we repeatedly do; excellence, then, is not an act but a habit." Whether standing watch on the bridge, in the central control station, at your console in the combat information center, or with boots on the deck of a ship you have just boarded, whether on duty, leave, or liberty, making excellence a habit is the truest path to success. This can happen only with a clear understanding of the captain's orders and intent, steadfast commitment to disciplined execution, and utmost respect for the covenant of trust, faith, and confidence shared between the captain and the officer.

I am proud of your decision to become a surface warfare officer. The work ahead is not easy; at times it will be frustrating and tough. I am convinced that by being the kind of leader from whom your shipmates can draw strength and inspiration, you can have a positive impact on your ship. After all, it is the impact you have on others, not the impact others have on you, that provides the greatest professional satisfaction. Ultimately, the respect and admiration reflected in the eyes of your shipmates are reward enough for your service, sacrifice, and commitment. I wish you fair winds and following seas.

—**CDR Vincent D. McBeth, USN (Ret.)**, completed tours in seven warships, including command of USS *McCampbell* (DDG 85) and USS *Tempest* (PC 2). Ashore, he served as administrative aide to the Secretary of the Navy; a White House Fellow; and special assistant to the Chairman of the Joint Chiefs of Staff and the Chief of Naval Operations. He holds a B.S. from the U.S. Naval Academy, an M.A. from The Fletcher School, and an M.S. from the National War College.

Appendix 1

Overview of the History of the U.S. Navy

The humble, halting birth of what would become the greatest Navy in history began when George Washington commissioned two armed vessels, at his own expense, in the fall of 1775 and ordered them to intercept British supply ships approaching the rebellious North American colonies. On 13 October the Continental Congress officially sanctioned Washington's actions and the Continental Navy was born.

By 1779 the mighty Royal Navy had all but swept the overmatched Continental Navy from the seas, but American privateers—privately funded and operating under official sanction from Congress—captured hundreds of British merchant ships, providing vital war supplies to the colonies and driving up the cost of shipping in Britain. The United States would return to this strategy of *guerre de course*, or war against commerce, again and again over the next two centuries. John Paul Jones—the most acclaimed naval figure of the Revolutionary War—fought his greatest battle just off the coast of England while attacking a British convoy of merchant ships, defeating HMS *Serapis* in the converted merchant ship *Bonhomme Richard*. Roaring the battle cry "I have not yet begun to fight!" while his ship was sinking beneath his feet, he battered the superior *Serapis* into submission and sailed her in triumph to a French port.

George Washington, reflecting on the war, wrote, "It follows then, as sure as night succeeds the day, that without a decisive naval force we can do nothing definitive—and with it, everything honorable and glorious." Despite General

Washington's urging, after the American victory at Yorktown the remaining units of the fleet were sold off, and the Navy ceased to exist in 1785. Without a navy to defend U.S. interests, American-owned merchant ships came under attack all over the world, particularly in Mediterranean waters, where the small kingdoms of the Barbary Coast had long preyed on passing vessels.

Recognizing the pressing need for a respectable navy, on 7 March 1794 Congress passed a bill authorizing the construction of six frigates. These vessels, including the immortal *Constitution*, were among the fastest and most powerful sailing frigates ever built, an early example of the long tradition of American technical prowess and innovation at sea. President Thomas Jefferson sent a four-ship squadron to the Mediterranean—the beginning of another long naval tradition of overseas presence. The war with the Barbary pirates that followed produced some of America's greatest naval heroes—names that grace the sterns of warships today: Preble, Bainbridge, Truxtun, and the indomitable Decatur.

The United States and Great Britain began a slide toward war again in 1807 when HMS *Leopard* attacked USS *Chesapeake* in her namesake body of water over the issue of naturalized American citizens who had emigrated (the British would say "deserted") from Britain. *Leopard* fired four broadsides into *Chesapeake* and seized four sailors from her crew, provoking nationwide outrage. In the first year of the War of 1812, American warships won a series of brilliant single-ship actions against the battle-hardened Royal Navy while USS *Essex*, under CAPT David Porter, ran wild in the Pacific and Indian Oceans, seizing British whalers and disrupting trade. In the American interior, Oliver Hazard Perry scratched together a fleet that swept the British from the Great Lakes at the Battle of Lake Erie (after the battle he tersely wrote, "We have met the enemy and they are ours"), while Thomas Macdonough's action on Lake Champlain was a decisive American victory that prevented a British advance out of Canada. The war sputtered to a halt in 1815 with the Treaty of Ghent.

Blockade, Brown Water, and the Birth of Modern Naval Warfare

During the Civil War from 1861 to 1865, the great preponderance of serving naval officers remained with the Union—less than one-fifth of the naval personnel serving in 1861 resigned to join the Confederacy (the greatest naval hero of the war, Union admiral David Farragut, was born in Alabama). Within days of the shelling of Fort Sumter a commerce war began in which the North attempted to strangle the Confederacy while the South attempted to disrupt northern sea trade with fast commerce raiders and to run supplies past Union squadrons blockading Confederate ports.

The Civil War was also the incubator of the modern U.S. Navy—indeed, of all modern naval warfare. Steam propulsion, armor, turreted guns, mines, and the submarine all appeared during this war. From an operational point of view, amphibious warfare, joint operations with the Army, and the application of industrial age production also emerged.

This technical revolution was on display when USS *Monitor* and CSS *Virginia* (more popularly known by her former Union name, *Merrimack*) met in March 1862 in the world's first battle between steam-powered ironclad ships. This battle on the waters of Hampton Roads, while inconclusive, previewed the future of naval warfare. In another historical first, CSS *Hunley* carried out a successful submarine attack, sinking USS *Husatonic* in Charleston harbor in 1864 (and incidentally sinking herself for the fourth time in the process).

By the final year of the Civil War, the Union Navy in close cooperation with the Army was tightening a noose around the South. The South's ports fell one by one. In August 1864 the Navy's first admiral, David Farragut, attacked Mobile, Alabama. Hanging off the rigging of his flagship USS *Harford* fully exposed to enemy fire in the midst of close-quarters battle, he ordered her to slew around the ship ahead with the cry, "Damn the torpedoes! Full speed ahead!" ("Torpedo" was the early name for a mine.) Mobile Bay was taken, leaving only one major port to the Confederacy. Later that year, ADM David Porter (son of the man who commanded *Essex* during the War of 1812) commanded a squadron that provided close gunfire support to advancing troops in an attack on Fort Fisher near Wilmington, North Carolina. More than two thousand Marines and Sailors participated in the combined-force assault, seizing the last major Confederate port.

The Navy emerged from the Civil War larger, battle-hardened, and ready to return to its worldwide responsibilities. By 1867 more than half the ships in commission were serving overseas.

Steam, Steel, Empire, and Global War

In the years following the Civil War the Navy began its usual peacetime decline in numbers and readiness, but it also experienced a technical and cultural revolution. Stephen Luce founded the Naval War College, and Alfred Thayer

Mahan wrote his masterwork, *The Influence of Sea Power upon History*, which profoundly affected naval thought for the next century. In 1895 the Navy's first true battleship, USS *Texas*, was commissioned. The United States would soon field a respectable battle fleet, even though the insular nation was still preoccupied with westward expansion within the North American continent.

In 1898, amid growing tension with Spain over the fate of Cuba, USS *Maine* exploded and sank in Havana harbor. Victory in the resulting war with Spain left the United States in possession of an unintentional overseas empire in the far western Pacific. The Navy played a dominant role in the Spanish-American War, crushing Spanish fleets at Santiago de Cuba and Manila Bay in the Philippines, the latter perhaps best remembered for Commodore Dewey's famous phrase, "You may fire when you are ready, Gridley."

With this lopsided victory and President Theodore Roosevelt's encouragement, the U.S. Navy became the emblem of a newly confident nation striding boldly onto the world stage. In 1907 Roosevelt sent the "Great White Fleet" on an around-the-world tour that underscored America's ascendancy. A few years earlier, in 1900, John Holland had launched the first practical submarine, inaugurating a new chapter in naval warfare, and in 1910 Eugene Eli flew the first aircraft from a ship, taking off from USS *Birmingham*. In the years that followed, the Navy grew in size, competence, and technical know-how, rivaling all but the British Royal Navy.

At the outbreak of World War I in 1914 the United States attempted to stay out of yet another European war while the Navy prepared. Provoked by Germany's unrestricted submarine warfare in the Atlantic, the United States finally declared war on 6 April 1917. In that same month German U-boats sank more than 800,000 tons of Allied shipping, pushing Britain to the brink of defeat. Help for the beleaguered British soon arrived in the form of a squadron of badly needed destroyers from the U.S. Navy. When the British asked how soon the Americans could be ready for sea, CDR Joseph Taussig promptly replied, "We are ready now," and the Navy entered the desperate struggle to keep the Allied lifelines open in the Atlantic.

Following the "war to end all wars," the Navy's capabilities diminished rapidly, victim of isolationist sentiment, the Great Depression, and an international treaty limiting the size of all major navies. Despite this, the Navy continued its tradition of innovation in peacetime, experimenting with carrier aviation (the Navy's first aircraft carrier, USS *Langley* [CV 1], was commissioned in 1922), replenishment at sea, and amphibious warfare. Submarines suitable for operating in the vast reaches of the Pacific Ocean were developed, radar made its appearance at sea, and antisubmarine sonar devices became a standard installation on escort vessels.

America's formal entry into World War II began with Japan's sneak attack on Pearl Harbor on 7 December 1941. Carrier-based Japanese dive-bombers and torpedo bombers destroyed the Navy's battle fleet, but the submarines were left untouched, as were the four fleet aircraft carriers out at sea. Broadly, the war in the Pacific can be divided into three phases: a Japanese offensive that conquered the Philippines, Singapore, and much of the western Pacific; a period of stalemate as Japanese and U.S. forces slugged it out in the south Pacific, particularly in the Solomon Islands; and the epic drive across the central Pacific that ended in the defeat of Japan. While the Pacific war raged, the Navy also fought the grim struggle against the U-boats in the Atlantic and built up the armadas that would land vast armies in North Africa, Sicily, Italy, and, on 6 June 1944, the beaches of Normandy, France.

The Pacific war was a naval war fought on a scale and with a ferocity not seen before or since. The initial period of bitter defeats ended in mid-1942 when Japan's advance toward New Guinea and Australia was checked at the Battle of Coral Sea (the first battle in history in which none of the opposing ships sighted each other). USS *Yorktown* (CV 5) suffered heavy bomb damage and limped back into Pearl Harbor to begin a projected three months of repairs. After less than three days of frantic work, Navy repair crews had her ready to put to sea to join USS *Enterprise* (CV 6) and USS *Hornet* (CV 8), then under the command of ADM Raymond Spruance, speeding toward Midway Island to meet the Japanese Combined Fleet. The resulting "miracle at Midway" comprised equal parts luck, superb intelligence work, and traditional American aggressive initiative in battle. Four Japanese carriers were sunk and their irreplaceable pilots killed, while only *Yorktown* was lost; the Japanese drive across the Pacific was halted.

Soon after Midway the United States went on the offensive with the invasion of Guadalcanal in the Solomon Islands. For months after the U.S. invasion, the fate of Guadalcanal remained uncertain. The Navy suffered tremendously as it learned night fighting the hard way, losing so many ships to Japanese torpedoes and guns that the waters off Guadalcanal became known as Iron Bottom Sound. When America's fortunes were at their lowest ebb, a new commander,

William "Bull" Halsey, was appointed, electrifying the Southwest Pacific Command. Halsey would go on to command the mighty Third Fleet, which led the drive on Japan, and he retired as one of only four five-star admirals (the others are Chester Nimitz, the Central Pacific commander in chief throughout the war; Ernest King, the CNO; and William Leahy, President Roosevelt's chief of staff).

Ashore on Guadalcanal, the U.S. Marines earned the first of a series of epic victories in a brutal island-hopping campaign that would take them all the way across the Pacific to Okinawa and Iwo Jima. The six-month seesaw fight in the southwest Pacific closed with future CNO Arleigh Burke's "perfect battle" at Cape St. George, a night destroyer fight that went entirely the U.S. Navy's way. The Navy paid a dear price in the Solomons campaign: after *Hornet* was sunk at the battle of Santa Cruz in October, the Americans in the southwest Pacific were down to a single, wounded carrier and one battleship. But within six months the Navy offensive was on an unstoppable roll. American production poured ships and aircraft into the Pacific theater even as the Allies landed in Italy and prepared for their storied surge across the English Channel. Also during this period the American submarine offensive, which began the day after the attack on Pearl Harbor with an order flashed across the Pacific to "execute unrestricted submarine warfare against Japan," was beginning to inflict devastating loses on Japanese merchant shipping. Eventually, VADM Charles A. Lockwood's small submarine force (less than 2 percent of active naval personnel) would strangle Japan's wartime economy, sinking 60 percent of all Japanese merchant shipping and 35 percent of Japan's warship tonnage.

The American drive across the Pacific steadily pushed back the Japanese defensive perimeter in 1944 and 1945 as one Japanese-occupied island after another fell. Titanic naval battles were fought, as at the Philippine Sea under Admiral Spruance—a battle so one-sided that VADM Marc Mitscher's carrier aviators dubbed it "the Great Marianas Turkey Shoot." The Battle of Leyte Gulf, fought when the Imperial Japanese Navy made a suicidal attempt to throw back the American invasion of the Philippines, involved more ships and men than any other naval battle in history. This battle featured the world's last battleship clash, in which ADM Jessie Oldendorf's old battleships—raised from the mud of Pearl Harbor—crushed a Japanese force advancing through Surigao Strait in the darkness, and Taffy 3's tiny escort carriers and destroyers fought a desperate battle against huge Japanese battleships off Samar later dubbed "the last stand of the Tincan Sailors." Taffy 3's small force had been left exposed when Halsey's Task Force 38 lunged north, taking the bait of the last Japanese carriers deliberately dangled in front of him. Inexplicably, with the hundreds of helpless transport ships practically under his guns, the Japanese commander turned back, apparently unnerved by the ferocity of the American destroyer attacks. After Leyte, the Imperial Navy ceased to exist as an effective fighting force, and the Japanese were forced to turn to a more desperate measure: the kamikaze.

The last chapter of the Navy's Pacific war was closed off Okinawa, a large Japanese home island with a population of almost half a million. Spruance's fast carrier force "came to stay" for forty days and nights, supporting Marines ashore and protecting the landing beaches, all the while within easy range of tens of thousands of Japanese aircraft. More than 4,900 Sailors lost their lives holding the line at Okinawa, victims of wave after wave of kamikaze attacks. Especially vulnerable were the gallant destroyers on radar picket duty on the fringes of the fleet. Many were sunk, and many more limped into port battered wrecks, barely afloat. The furious kamikaze onslaught at Okinawa was Japan's last death spasm: a scant three months later, USS *Missouri* led the fleet into Tokyo Bay to accept Japan's unconditional surrender. The Navy achieved its most lasting glory in the Pacific campaign of World War II, and the great drive across the Pacific occupies the very center of the U.S. Navy's cultural identity to this day.

Limited Wars and Cold War

Continuing the Navy's tradition of innovation in peacetime, some of the world's best engineers and leaders brought revolutionary advancements to the postwar fleet: nuclear-powered submarines, ballistic missiles, and the technical revolution that led to the familiar Aegis combat system at the heart of the modern surface combatant. Nuclear propulsion and jet aircraft were married in USS *Enterprise*, the first nuclear-powered super-carrier.

Operationally, the Navy prepared to fight the Soviet Union at sea, most notably during the blockade of Cuba in the 1962 Cuban Missile Crisis and in the 1980s Reagan-era buildup to the six-hundred-ship Navy, which was designed to challenge the Soviets on their front doorstep. While preparing for blue-water conflict with the USSR, the Navy also participated in a series of limited wars and worked to prevent others. Navy aircraft flew thousands of missions during the Korean and Vietnam Wars. Among the heroes who emerged from Vietnam, John McCain, VADM James Stockdale, and VADM William P. Lawrence are representative of the hundreds of naval aviators shot down over North Vietnam who would return with honor after enduring years of brutality in North Vietnamese prison camps. Navy riverine squadrons fought on the Mekong Delta, reprising the brown-water mission from the Civil War, and surface units spent weeks on gun lines providing fire support to troops ashore. During the later years of this conflict, CNO Elmo Zumwalt initiated a series of long-overdue reforms to personnel and management policies that created the foundation for today's all-volunteer, highly professional Navy.

Carrier aircraft played vital roles in Operations Desert Storm, Enduring Freedom, and Iraqi Freedom, while the surface Navy added a new capability with precision-strike Tomahawk land attack missiles. In a demonstration of the Navy's inherent flexibility and warfighting readiness, warships arrived in the North Arabian Sea the day after the 11 September 2001 attacks on the World Trade Center and the Pentagon. The Navy contributed the lion's share of the combat power that took down the Taliban regime in only five weeks. The rapid deployment of more than fifty ships to the North Arabian Sea in the month after 9/11 contrasts with the sustained deployments necessary to support combat operations in Iraq and Syria. Throughout these limited wars, thousands of Navy personnel have served on the ground in Iraq and Afghanistan, including the elite Navy SEALs who famously killed Osama bin Laden during a daring raid into Pakistan in May 2011, almost ten years after he masterminded the 9/11 attacks.

Throughout the U.S. Navy's history, certain threads bind the saga together: aggressive initiative in battle, technical innovation, joint operations with other services, and forward-deployed operations around the world. On the bridges of warships, in the cockpits of aircraft, beneath the seas, and in hotspots ashore around the world, the story continues today.

—**James Rushton** is a retired surface warfare officer with more than thirty-two years of active service. A former limited duty officer and enlisted submariner, he served sea tours in eight warships, including command of USS *Dextrous* (MCM 13). He holds a master's degree in national security analysis from the Naval Postgraduate School.

Appendix 2

Useful Websites

The Internet is a major source of information, communication, and entertainment for most of us who have earned a commission since 2000. Our first instinct when confronted with an information need is to "google" it; but it is very important to remember that online content is easily manipulated and sometimes flat-out wrong. The Internet is a tool to help you search and learn, but there is no substitute for conducting original research and thinking for yourself.

With that caveat in mind, the Internet remains a valuable tool that will help you navigate your life at work and home. Listed below under several categories are a few websites that are particularly relevant to a newly minted junior officer—particularly those with no prior military experience. As you browse these sites you will find that their content does not necessarily reflect the opinions of the U.S. Navy. In fact, our inclusion of these sites does not constitute an endorsement of the products, services, or opinions you may encounter as you visit them, but this list represents the sites that many junior officers visit as they manage their lives in the Navy.

Career

- Navy Personnel Command, http://www.public.navy.mil/bupers-npc/Pages/default.aspx
- BUPERS Online, https://www.bol.navy.mil

The Navy Personnel Command (NPC) site has your detailer's contact information, slates, board information, community information, and much, much more. NPC contains a lot of important material including critical information on promotion and screening boards, links to detailers, plus you can view any All Navy (ALNAV) or Naval Administration (NAVADMIN) message released since 2000. BUPERS Online contains all of your career information and qualifications in your officer data card as well as your fitness report history.

Professional Development and Education

- My Navy Portal, http://my.navy.mil
- Navy Professional Reading Program, http://www.navy.mil/ah_online/cno-readingprogram
- Navy MWR Digital Library, https://mwrdigitallibrary.navy.mil
- Naval History and Heritage Command, www.history.navy.mil

My Navy Portal (MNP), formerly Navy Knowledge Online, is the new home for Navy e-learning, your electronic training jacket, career tools, online courses, and more. MNP requires a common access card (CAC) to log in. It is continually populated with tools for you and your Sailors, and you will be routinely required to complete MNP courses related to various programs and subjects that the Navy deems important. The Navy Professional Reading Program site, covered in more detail in appendix 3, contains several book collections along with a synopsis of each book. The Navy MWR Digital Library is also a CAC-enabled site that provides you with free access to download digital magazines, newspapers, and many of the recommended e-books and audio books. Finally, the Naval History and Heritage Command website is a terrific site to research naval history topics.

Family Readiness and Relocation

- Ready.Gov, www.ready.gov
- Commander Navy Installations Command, https://www.cnic.navy.mil
- Move.mil, www.move.mil
- Navy Exchange (NEX) Moving Guide, https://www.mynavyexchange.com/assets/Static/Moving/MovingGuide.pdf
- Defense Travel Management Office, http://www.defensetravel.dod.mil

- Great Schools, http://www.greatschools.net/
- Facebook, www.facebook.com

Family readiness in the face of disaster is critical for Navy families who may be without their Sailor or in a new community. Ready.gov ensures that families are prepared for an emergency. The Commander Navy Installations Command (CNIC) site includes a number of links related to family readiness, including one to the Ready Navy Emergency Response Program, the Navy's site for family emergency readiness.

Relocation is also a way of life in the military. A number of websites can help reduce the time, stress, and confusion of permanent change of station (PCS) moves and temporary duty (TDY) travel. The CNIC site provides installation information that you may find helpful. Move.mil, a Defense Personal Property website, allows members or their spouses to coordinate their household goods move. The NEX Moving Guide is a checklist to help you prepare for an upcoming PCS move. The Defense Travel Management site is a clearinghouse for questions regarding per diem, basic allowance for housing (BAH), and travel or moves. Great Schools is an award-winning website that includes research, ratings, and testimonials for K–12 schools across the country. Finally, there are numerous Facebook groups that offer support to families who are new to a command or region.

Service-Related News and Entertainment

- U.S. Navy official website, www.navy.mil
- U.S. Navy Chief of Information—Navy News Desk, http://www.navy.mil/local/chinfo/
- Military.com, www.military.com
- *Navy Times*, www.navytimes.com
- Naval Institute Press, www.usni.org
- U.S. Navy Social Media Index, http://www.navy.mil/Command Directory.asp

To stay connected to the broader Navy, visit the Navy's official website regularly or the Navy's Chief of Information site. Military.com has a wide variety of information and links for all members of the military, including pay and benefits, educational opportunities, military discounts, and current events. *Navy Times* is an unaffiliated Navy-specific website that is widely read for late-breaking news and commentary on important happenings. The Naval Institute Press is an independent forum that produces thoughtful periodicals, scholarly books, and stimulating conferences. Finally, most commands use a variety of social media platforms including Facebook, Twitter, and YouTube to share information with Sailors and their families. A complete listing is posted on the U.S. Navy's Social Media Index website. There are also numerous Facebook groups that are not officially sanctioned by the Navy but provide mentorship and networking opportunities. With their wealth of information and links, these sites are a great starting point for the latest in what is going on in the fleet—especially when you are out of the loop on deployment or on shore duty.

Community Sites and Blogs

- U.S. Naval Institute Blog, https://blog.usni.org
- Naval Supply Systems Command (NAVSUP) homepage, https://www.navsup.navy.mil/public/navsup/home/
- Sailor Bob, www.sailorbob.com/phpBB2/index.php
- CDR Salamander, http://cdrsalamander.blogspot.com/
- Center for International Maritime Security, http://cimsec.org
- War on the Rocks, https://warontherocks.com
- Air Warriors, www.airwarriors.com

Professionals in the arenas of politics, business, and sports seek out information from a combination of sources both official and informal, and naval officers are no exception. Among the more professionally managed Internet sites that you may find useful is the U.S. Naval Institute Blog, which covers a variety of topics spanning all warfare communities. NAVSUP has a direct link to the online version of the *Supply Corps Newsletter*, the My Navy Portal Supply Corps officers page, and instructions on how to access the Naval Logistics Library (NLL).

In addition to the official sites, some blogs have both entertaining and informative posts that help the reader gain perspective and insights from members in their own and other communities. SailorBob, CDR Salamander, Center for International Maritime Security, War on the Rocks, and AirWarriors are not officially affiliated with the military and are the electronic equivalent of talking with a large group of peers around the water cooler. Just like real-life water-cooler conversations, not everything you read on these sites may align with Navy policy and opinion, but it is foolish to ignore these sources of information and discussion just because they are not official sites.

Financial Sites

- United Services Automobile Association, www.usaa.com
- Navy Federal Credit Union, www.navyfcu.org
- Mint.com, www.mint.com
- MyPay.com, https://mypay.dfas.mil/mypay.aspx
- Thrift Savings Plan, http://www.tsp.gov/index.html
- Blended Retirement System, http://militarypay.defense.gov/Blended Retirement/

Although a wide array of financial service sites is available on the World Wide Web, USAA and NFCU are two financial institutions that have enjoyed long-standing relationships with Navy personnel. Mint.com is an award-winning site that helps you track your spending and investments, breaks your spending down into easy-to-understand charts and graphs, and helps you budget your money. MyPay.com gives you access to your leave and earnings statements, W-2, and other pay-related links. The Thrift Savings Plan (TSP) and Blended Retirement sites give you access to your government investment contributions as well as detailed information about the Navy's new retirement system.

Navy Family Support

- Fleet and Family Support Center, https://cnic.navy.mil/ffr/family_readiness/fleet_and_family_support_program.html
- Military OneSource, https://www.militaryonesource.mil
- Military Spouse, http://militaryspouse.com
- Military.com Discount Page, http://shock.military.com/DC/Deal Index.jsp
- The Military Family Network, http://www.emilitary.org/index.html

There are a number of resources to help support Navy families. While the Fleet and Family Support Center and Military OneSource websites are a great place to start, there are many sites such as the Military Spouse website that offer programs of support for Navy families. Additionally, there are a number of sites focused on providing military family members discounts or access to services. The discount page on Military.com allows users and merchants to list military specials. It also has a sort function that allows users to search for deals where they live. The Military Family Network site is a portal that links you to virtually all types of benefits, services, healthcare, employment opportunities, and more.

The Internet has changed our society, and the Navy is no exception. As is the case with advice from your peers and more traditional media sources, you will be best served by seeking out information from a number of sources rather than relying solely on one source for all of your information. Nevertheless, the web is here to stay, and you should leverage that tool to the fullest in your journey as a newly commissioned officer.

—Compiled and written by **LCDR Micah Murphy**, **LCDR Rob Niemeyer**, and **LCDR Samantha O'Neil**.

Appendix 3

The Chief of Naval Operations Professional Reading Program . . . and Beyond

The Chief of Naval Operations Professional Reading Program (CNO PRP) was designed and launched in 2006 to encourage service members to enhance their personal and professional development through a variety of popular and readily accessible books. The program has evolved over the years, and the suggested readings are now categorized to align with the current CNO, ADM John M. Richardson, and his Lines of Effort and tenets as outlined in *A Design for Maintaining Maritime Superiority* (http://www.navy.mil/cno/docs/CNO_STG1.pdf). The CNO, working with a cross-section of military and academic professionals, carefully crafted an extensive list of books broken into six sections: The Canon, Core Attributes, Naval Power, Fast Learning, Navy Team, and Partnerships. The books include traditional topics such as leadership, military heritage, and joint warfare and then extend beyond military issues to incorporate cultural awareness, critical thinking, and management theory from the business world. The collections are geared toward enhancing your leadership development, and there are terrific books on each list that you should certainly consider reading.

Why Should I Participate?

As a newly commissioned officer, your days (and nights) will be full as you try to balance job responsibilities, the pursuit of important warfare qualifications, family obligations, and a personal life. Among all these legitimate pursuits, however, reading is one that will replenish your mind with new ideas and new ways to look at the world. There is no requirement to delve into this program, but you may be left on the sidelines of some great discussions among your coworkers if you opt to forgo reading as you progress in the Navy. There are many benefits to being a lifelong learner. Reading the books on these lists can help you gain insight into:

- The history of the naval service
- Leadership principles from fictional and historical figures
- Significant historical events
- Behavioral and cultural differences
- Parallels to the business world
- Diverse perspectives on a variety of issues

If the above reasons are not enough, reading is also a proven way to relieve the stress of everyday life and work. It provides an escape from reality, even if just for a few minutes. If you are in an operational command in particular, reading a few pages of a favorite book before turning in is one of the true small pleasures of life at sea.

How Does It Work?

The CNO PRP groups more than one hundred books into separate collections, each supporting one of the CNO's Lines of Effort. The extensive lists can be located at http://www.navy.mil/ah_online/cno-readingprogram/ (or google "CNO Professional Reading Program").

Below is a brief sample of books taken from the CNO PRP website for you to consider. As you review this list, visit the website on your own to see if other books strike your interest.

The Canon

These books provide fundamental knowledge of the naval profession, history, and strategy.

- *Masters of War: Classical Strategic Thought* by Michael I. Handel
- *Military Strategy: A General Theory of Power Control* by J. C. Wylie

- *The Influence of Sea Power upon History: 1660–1783* by Alfred T. Mahan
- *Principles of Maritime Strategy* by Julian S. Corbett
- *The Art of War* by Sun Tzu

Core Attributes

These books highlight how integrity, accountability, initiative, and toughness guide leaders in their decision-making and action-taking processes.

- *Leaders Eat Last: Why Some Teams Pull Together and Others Don't* by Simon Sinek
- *Make Your Bed: Little Things That Can Change Your Life and Maybe the World* by ADM William H. McRaven
- *Matterhorn: A Novel of the Vietnam War* by Karl Marlantes
- *The 7 Signs of Ethical Collapse* by Marianne M. Jennings
- *Warriors and Citizens: American Views of our Military* by Kori Schake and Jim Mattis

Naval Power

These books aim to increase knowledge about classic and modern maritime strategy while reinforcing historical lessons learned.

- *Master and Commander* by Patrick O'Brian
- *Sea Power: The History and Geopolitics of the World's Oceans* by ADM James Stavridis
- *Six Frigates: The Epic History of the Founding of the U.S. Navy* by Ian Toll
- *The Last Stand of the Tin Can Sailors: The Extraordinary World War II Story of the U.S. Navy's Finest Hour* by James D. Hornfischer
- *The Rules of the Game: Jutland and British Naval Command* by Andrew Gordon

Fast Learning

Books in this section focus on ways leaders can improve how they absorb and process information in order to execute sound and timely decisions.

- *Execution: The Discipline of Getting Things Done* by Larry Bossidy and Ram Charan
- *Freakonomics: A Rogue Economist Explores the Hidden Side of Everything* by Steven Levitt and Stephen Dubner
- *High-Velocity Edge: How Market Leaders Leverage Operational Excellence* by Steven J. Spear
- *Innovator's Dilemma: The Revolutionary Book That Will Change the Way You Do Business* by Clayton Christensen
- *Thinking, Fast and Slow* by Daniel Kahneman

Navy Team

The Navy is comprised of Sailors from all backgrounds and experiences. Books in this section highlight the importance of leveraging individual strengths and embracing diversity to create operational excellence.

- *Teams of Teams: New Rules of Engagement for a Complex World* by Stanley McChrystal
- *The Accidental Admiral: A Sailor Takes Command at NATO* by James Stavridis
- *Thoughts of a Philosophical Fighter Pilot* by Jim Stockdale
- *The Tipping Point: How Little Things Can Make a Big Difference* by Malcolm Gladwell
- *Tribe: On Homecoming and Belonging* by Sebastian Junger

Partnerships

These books illustrate the importance of forging and deepening operational relationships, domestically and internationally, in order to strengthen our naval power.

- *At Ease: Stories I Tell to Friends* by Dwight D. Eisenhower
- *Grand Strategies in War and Peace* by Paul Kennedy
- *The Paradox of American Power: Why the World's Only Superpower Can't Go It Alone* by Joseph S. Nye Jr.
- *The Revenge of Geography: What the Map Tells Us about Coming Conflicts and the Battle against Fate* by Robert D. Kaplan
- *World Order* by Henry Kissinger

Other Notable Selections
- *A Sailor's History of the U.S. Navy* by Thomas Cutler
- *Ender's Game* by Orson Scott Card
- *One Hundred Years of Sea Power: The U.S. Navy, 1890–1990* by George Baer
- *The Cruel Sea* by Nicholas Monsarrat
- *The Golden Thirteen: Recollections of the First Black Naval Officers* edited by Paul Stillwell; foreword by Colin Powell
- *The Good Shepherd* by C. S. Forester
- *The Leader's Bookshelf* by James Stavridis and R. Manning Ancell
- *Two Souls Indivisible: The Friendship That Saved Two POWs in Vietnam* by James Hirsch

Where Do I Find These Books?
- Your unit's library (each command has been given a full set)
- Base library
- Your local public library
- The Navy Exchange (or https://www.mynavyexchange.com)
- U.S. Naval Institute Press (www.usni.org)—offers discounts for members
- Other online book sellers such as Amazon or Barnes and Noble

Other ways to access these selections are to download them to your computer as e-books or listen to them as audio books. The CNO PRP website provides a direct link to the Navy General Library Program (https://navy.libraryreserve.com/10/50/en/Default.htm). Here you can either log in using your CAC or create a Department of Defense Self-Service Logon (DS Logon) account. You can also access both the Navy General Library Program and MWR Digital Library (https://mwrdigitallibrary.navy.mil) through the My Navy Portal (https://my.navy.mil/) website. Within each application you can search for books on the CNO PRP list and listen to or read them on your personal computer or mobile device.

What Does the Future Hold for the Navy Reading Program?
Since its debut in the fall of 2006, the reading program has been extremely successful and continues to have strong commitment from the CNO. While

the book selection committee aims to pick "timeless" books for the collection, there are periodic reviews every eighteen to twenty-four months, so don't be surprised to see minor changes from time to time. Finally, keep your eye out for new technological avenues to deliver books to Sailors (other than e-books and audio books) to accommodate different learning styles.

Other Avenues to Accelerate Your Mind

The list above provides a wide range of superb books, but there are other reading sources available to broaden your mind.

Recommended Publications

The Economist. Published weekly, this magazine reports on worldwide events and topics that include politics, public policy, finance, and foreign relations. If you have time to read only one magazine a week, consider this one. If this magazine is not your cup of tea, consider reading another weekly news magazine such as *Time* for an efficient way to keep up with current events.

Foreign Affairs. Published quarterly (print and online at www.cfr.org), the Council of Foreign Relations' nonpartisan information and analysis are great assets to understanding what is going on in the world and our potential role in shaping its future.

U.S. Naval Institute *Proceedings.* Published monthly by the U.S. Naval Institute and billed as "The Independent Forum on National Defense," the *Proceedings* contains valuable insight, news, and advice for sea service professionals.

Harvard Business Review (https://hbr.org). Topics include leadership, high-performance management, managing projects, and effective communication.

Recommended Podcasts

Leadership: Center for Creative Leadership (http://www.ccl.org/leadership/pod.xml)

Navy: CNO Podcast, Navy–Marine Corps Radio News (http://www.navy.mil/podcast/podcast.asp)

Leadership and Character in the Movies

Although many of the best movies focused on military leadership were produced in the early post–World War II era, some more recent movies also explore the concepts of leadership and character. These films use both positive and negative examples and would be good candidates for individual viewing or for a professional movie night with your wardroom.

Military Leadership
- *We Were Soldiers*
- *Saving Private Ryan*
- *Master and Commander*
- *Glory*
- *Patton*
- *The Great Escape*
- *Gladiator*
- *Gettysburg*
- *Hacksaw Ridge*

Sports and Teamwork
- *Miracle*
- *Remember the Titans*
- *Rudy*
- *Hoosiers*
- *Invictus*

Organizational Behavior
- *12 Angry Men*
- *Conspiracy*
- *Glengarry Glen Ross*
- *The Big Short*

—Compiled and written by **LCDR Micah Murphy**, **LCDR Rob Niemeyer**, and **LCDR Samantha O'Neil**.

Index

abbreviations, xv–xix
accountability, 2, 130
administration: anticipation, planning, and meeting deadlines, 85–86, 95; attention to detail in paperwork, 84, 95, 137; awards management and administration, 91–93; classified material, 90, 93–95; consequences of neglect of, 84; counseling requirements, 90–91; disciplinary proceedings, 91; duties and responsibilities related to, 84–85; e-mail etiquette, 88–90; importance of, 84–85, 95; paperwork completion and all-but-the-signature standard, 85; performance evaluations, 90–91, 93; point paper, 87–88; references library, 93; references/instructions for documents, 87; repetitive requirements and templates for products, 87; review of reports and documents, 137; tickler for tracking requirements and deadlines, 86, 93; time management and, 84–85, 152–55; writing style and proofreading for clarity, 86–87
aerospace engineering duty officer, 110
Afghanistan operations, 170
Air Force Air Mobility Command (AMC), 56
alcohol use and abuse, 80–81, 150
alcohol-related incidents (ARIs), 80
allowances, 61, 62

all-volunteer force, transition to, 170
American Red Cross and AMCROSS messages, 57–58
Aristotle, 162
assessments (inspections), 132
attitudes and success, 1–2
aviation career paths, 97, 99–100
aviation engineering duty officers, 102
awards, personal and command, 91–93

balls, 115–16
Barbary war, 164
benefits, 64–67
billet, 19
blogs, 174–75
Bluejacket's Manual, The (Cutler), 31, 32
body composition assessment (BCA), 78–79
bonus pay, 61–62
books and references: advice books for spouses, 112; career information, 111; etiquette reference, 41; management references, 124, 126; movies, 183; naval customs and traditions, 31; Navy mission, goals and direction policy documents, 71–72; periodicals, 182; podcasts, 182; PQS books (cards), 23; professional library recommendations, 31, 93; Professional Reading Program, 172, 177–82; warfare-specific publications and manuals, 133

books and references/instructions: awards instruction and manual, 92; instructions and naval references to guide events and activities, 12–13; program instructions and publications, 131; references/instructions for documents, 87, 93
briefs, tactical, 133
BUPERS Online (BOL), 109
Bureau of Naval Personnel (BUPERS), 16, 102, 109, 111, 171–72
burial-at-sea ceremonies, 36
Burke, Arleigh, 24, 168

Captain's Mast, 91
career: detailer and detailing process, 97; focus on job at hand, future opportunities will fall in place, 2; line officers, 97–104; long-term goals and planning for future, 2, 96; performance expectations and traits, 10, 107–9; professional benefits of socializing in the wardroom, 42; references, 111; references and website resources, 171–72; restricted line officers, 98, 105–7; service record management, 108–9; superior performance and promotion opportunities, 97, 107, 110; typical career paths, 98–101; understanding opportunities and promotion, 96
Career Compass (Winnefeld), 111
Career Intermission Program, 81
certifications, 132
chain of command: at naval schools, 140–42; shipboard organization, 24, 25–26
change-of-command ceremonies, 36
Chaplain Corps, 105
character/military bearing and conduct: alcohol and drug abuse, 80–81, 150; awareness of problems and helping before crises occur, 12; conduct while attending naval schools, 149–50; counseling requirements, 90–91; misconduct and punishment, 80, 91; motivation, intellect, and personal example, 160–62; movie examples, 183; performance expectations and traits, 10; UCMJ violations and punishment, 91
charitable causes, 82–83
checklists (check sheets), 135, 136
Chief of Naval Operations Professional Reading Program (CNO PRP): access to books, 181; background of, 177; benefits of participation, 177–78; sample of collections, 178–81; success of and future of, 181–82; website for, 172, 178
chief petty officer (CPO), 8, 27–28, 128
chief warrant officers (CWOs), 104, 107
child and domestic abuse, 77
christening ceremonies, 36–37
Civil Engineer Corps (CEC) officers, 106–7, 110
Civil War and birth of modern Navy, 164–65
classified material: classification levels, 93–94; definition of, 93; e-mail and handling of, 90; guidance on handling of, 93–95; naval school security and, 147; need to know and sharing of, 94–95; secure areas for working with, 94, 95; security awareness briefings, 94
clothing: civilian clothing, 48–49, 54; sponsor advice on clothing and other needs, 30. *See also* uniforms
code of social ethics, 50
Cold War, 169–70
collaboration at sea (CAS) site, 133
collateral duties, 129–30, 135
colors, morning and evening, 34
combat readiness and execution, 161
Combined Federal Campaign (CFC) program, 82–83
command awards, 93
command duty officer (CDO), 26
command financial specialist (CFS), 63–64
command managed equal opportunity (CMEO) manager, 73–74
command master chief (CMC), 58, 117
command master chief (CMC) spouse, 117
command ombudsman, 58, 76–77, 118
commander of naval school, 141–42
commanding officer (CO): chain of command, 25; change-of-command ceremonies, 36; courtesies for interacting with, 35, 116; duties and responsibilities of, 116; letter to new, 18–19; official calls custom, 39–40; philosophy, vision, and expectations of, 22, 72, 152; relationship protocol and traditions, 27; visits in other ports, escort or driving duties during, 40
commanding officer (CO) spouse, 117

Index ◆ 187

commanding officers, advice from: become the master of your craft, 156; claim ownership and make things happen, 157; intellectual curiosity, 157; maturity, 159; motivation, intellect, and personal example, 160–62; never wait to make a difference, 155–58; passion, 159; SEAL team officer performance expectations and traits, 158–60; teams, leadership style, and managing relationships, 158–59; time management, 152–55; trust, 159–60; warship officer performance expectations and traits, 160–62
command/organizational climate, 10
commissioning ceremonies, 36–37
commitment, 69–71
communication: alternatives to e-mail, 89; daily intention messages (DIMs), 133; e-mail etiquette, 88–90; e-mail to spouse and family, 120–21; keep the chain of command informed, 25; message traffic, 133; military family communications, 120–21; misinterpretation of messages, 89; phone calls/voice communications, 120, 121; social media, 28–29, 75–76, 173, 174; before you report to new command, 14, 19. *See also* correspondence
community relations (COMREL) projects, 82
conduct. *See* character/military bearing and conduct
Cooperative Strategy for 21st Century Seapower, A, 72
core values, 9, 69–71
correspondence: e-mail etiquette, 88–90; first impressions made through, 18; letter to new commanding officer, 18–19; manual for guidance on, 87; misinterpretation of messages, 89; thank-you notes, 47–48; turnover letter, 126–27
Correspondence Manual, 87, 93
counseling requirements, 90–91
courage: core values, 69–71; leadership and requirement for, 6
crossing-the-line ceremonies, 38
customs and traditions: attention to detail and adherence to, 32; books about, 31; ceremonies and events, 36–40; colors, morning and evening, 34; foreign customs, 40; greetings, 32–33; importance and strength of service from, 26, 31, 40; national anthem and ensign, 33–34; quarterdeck, 33; saluting, 32–33, 34, 35; seniors, interacting with, 35; shipboard and naval protocol, 26–29; wardroom etiquette, 22, 34–35

daily intention messages (DIMs), 133
Defense, Department of: *DoD Manual of Military Decorations and Awards*, 92; Safe Helpline, 74–75
Defense Finance Accounting Service (DFAS), 61
Defense Information School (DINFOS), 104
Defense Language Institute (DLI), 104
dental care, 64–65
Dental Corps, 105–6
department heads, 24–25, 27, 117–18, 134
dependent identification cards, 119
deployment: assessment outcomes and delay in, 132; definition of, 113; plan of action and milestones (POA&M) for preparations for, 136; separations and reunions, 121–22; support and assistance during, 67
Design for Maintaining Maritime Security, A (Richardson), 71–72, 177
detailer and detailing process, 97
dining in, 38–39
dining out, 39
discharge for alcohol-related incidents, 80
dissent/loyal dissent, 9
Division in the Spotlight (DITS) program and inspection, 138
division officer: assignment as, 12, 24, 25; duties and responsibilities of, 24–25, 128–30; growing on the job, 130; leadership and management skills for, 24; managing up, 134; quality of work, responsibility for, 137–38; reenlistment ceremonies and selection as reenlisting officer, 38; relationship protocol and traditions, 26–29, 130; success as, 130. *See also* administration; management responsibilities
division officer notebook, 6–7
Division Officer's Guide, 24, 93
DoD Manual of Military Decorations and Awards, 92
domestic and child abuse, 77
drug abuse, 80
drug and alcohol prevention advisor (DAPA), 80

duty assignment, first: apprehension about, 15; become the master of your craft, 156; chain of command, 24, 25–26; check-in process, 21; communication before you report to new command, 14, 19; first day at, 20–22; first few weeks at, 22–26; letter to new commanding officer, 18–19; meal on first day, 22; orders for, 16, 17; relationship protocol and traditions, 26–29; reporting to and how to get to first command, 19–20; settling in, 30; sponsor for, 16–18, 21, 22, 30; training for, 3; uniform for reporting to, 21; before you report, 14–15
duty section assignments, 26

education: advanced degrees, 66–67, 108; joint professional military education (JPME), 108; professional development and, 139–40, 151; tuition assistance, 66–67; website resources, 172. *See also* schools, naval
Education and Training Placement resource, 108
e-mail: etiquette for, 88–90; military family communications, 120–21
emergency planning and response, 118–19
Emily Post's Etiquette (Post and Senning), 42
engineering duty officers (EDOs), 97, 102, 110
engineering officer of the watch (EOOW), 23, 26
Equal Opportunity (EO) program and policy, 73–74
equator, ceremonies for crossing, 38
etiquette/social etiquette: consideration and respect in social interactions, 41, 46, 50; hosting or organizing an event, 44–45; introductions at events, 49; invitations, responding to, 46, 116; learning rules of, 41–42; meals and table manners, 43–44; references on, 41–42; social and personal conduct, 46–47; socializing and entertaining, 42–43; thank-you notes, 47–48; tipping, 49
evening colors, 34
excellence as a habit, 162
executive officer (XO), 18, 25, 27, 117
Executive Officer Inquiry (XOI), 91
exercises, message traffic about, 133
explosive ordnance officers (EODs), 101

families. *See* spouses and families
Family Advocacy Program (FAP), 77
Family Care Plan (FCP), 81
family days, 120
Family Readiness Group, 115
Farragut, David, 164, 165
fatigue and sleep, 79, 150
finances: benefits, 64–67; counseling about, 64, 67; emergency leave and funds for travel, 58; experience and knowledge of sailors about, 63; helping sailors avoid problems with, 63–64, 68; home loan benefit, 67; pay and allowances, 60–63; sailors in financial distress, 64; security clearances and financial problems, 64; training on, 63–64, 67; website resources, 175
fitness report (FITREP), 10, 109
Fleet and Family Support Center (FFSC), 64, 67, 76–77, 175
Fleet Industrial Supply Centers (FISCs), 106
foreign area officers (FAOs), 97, 104, 110
foreign customs, 40
fraternization policy, 75
full-time support (FTS) officers, 102, 110

Golden Rule, 9
Goldwater-Nichols Defense Reorganization Act, 108
Great White Fleet tour, 166
greetings customs, 32–33

Hail and Farewell gatherings, 39, 47, 114–15
Halsey, William "Bull," 168, 169
hard work and success, 1–2
hazing, 38
history of the Navy: Afghanistan operations, 170; Barbary war, 164; birth of the Navy, 163–64; Civil War and birth of modern Navy, 164–65; Cold War and limited wars, 169–70; decline of Navy during peacetime, 163–64, 165, 166; Great White Fleet tour, 166; innovation during peacetime, 165–67, 169; Iraq operations, 170; policy reforms and transition to all-volunteer force, 170; Spanish-American War, 166; Vietnam War, 169–70; War of 1812, 164; World War I, 166; World War II, 167–69
home loan benefit, VA, 67
Homefront Club (Eckart), 112

honor, 69–71
human resource (HR) officers, 102–3, 110
humility, 7

identification cards, 119
indoctrination (Indoc), 22
Influence of Sea Power upon History (Mahan), 166, 179
information professional officers (IPs), 103, 110
information warfare officers (IWs), 103, 110
inspections (assessments), 132
instructions. *See* books and references/instructions
instructors, 142
integrity, 6
intellectual curiosity, 157
intelligence officers (IOs), 101, 103, 110
introductions at events, 49
invitations, responding to, 46, 116
Iraq operations, 170

Jefferson, Thomas, 164
Joint Federal Travel Regulations (JFTR), 54
joint professional military education (JPME), 108
judge advocate generals (JAGs), 105

khaki call, 128
King, Ernest, 168
Krongard, Alex, 158–60

Lawrence, William P., 170
leadership/leaders: authentic and best self, 4; best performance expectations, 13; constructive criticism and negative feedback, skills for delivery of, 5–6; courage requirements, 6; development and promotion of core values by, 71; divisional leadership positions and responsibilities, 128–30; early opportunities for, 12; feelings about first leadership opportunities, 3; following your leaders, 8–9, 161; forward-looking focus of, 8; humility and respect for others, 7; integrity of leaders, 6; motivation, intellect, and personal example, 160–62; movie examples, 183; performance expectations and traits, 10, 152–62; personal example and leading by example, 3–4, 161–62; punctuality/timeliness and respect for others, 4, 10–11; relationship and partnership with senior enlisted leadership, 8; standard-setting and performance expectations, 5; taking charge and commanding organization, 4–5; teams, leadership style, and managing relationships, 158–59; training for and learning skills, 3, 24; vision statements, 71; walking around and engagement with sailors, 7; warfighting and operational competence focus, 5
leading chief petty officer (LCPO), 25, 129, 130, 137
leading petty officer (LPO), 8, 25, 128, 129
Leahy, William, 168
leave: accrual and accumulation of, 51–52; emergency leave, 52, 57–58; naval school attendance and, 147–48; normal leave, 56–57; requests for and approval of, 52, 56–58, 59, 114
leave and earnings statement (LES), 62
liberty, 51, 52–53, 58–59, 114, 147–48
life insurance, 65
life/work balance and retention initiatives, 81
limited duty officers (LDOs), 104, 107
limited wars, 169–70
line officers, 97–104
Lines of Effort, 177, 178
Luce, Stephen, 165

Macdonough, Thomas, 164
Mahan, Alfred Thayer, 165–66
maintenance, material, and management system (3M), 137
maintenance personnel, 129
maintenance spot checks, 137
"majoring on the major issues," 138
management responsibilities: assessments and certifications, 132; challenges and rewards of, 138; checklists, 135, 136; collateral duties, 129–30, 135; delegation of responsibilities, 128; division, management of, 128–30; divisional leadership positions and responsibilities, 128–30; growing on the job, 130; maintenance spot checks, 137; managing up, 134; morning meetings, 128; plan of action and milestones (POA&M) tool, 136; planning and executing tasks, 135–36; program management, 130–31; quality of work, responsibility for,

137–38; questions, clarifying guidance, and doing own research, 134; references for requirements and procedures, 124, 126, 131; self-critical focus to find and fix problems, 136; tactical preparations and responsibilities, 133; time management and, 135, 152–55; turnover of responsibilities, 124–27
maritime power strategy document, 72
maternity leave policy, 82
maturity, 159
McBeth, Vincent D., 160–62
McCain, John, 170
McGrath, Bryan, 152–55
meals and table manners, 43–44
medical care, 64–65
Medical Corps, 105–6
Medical Service Corps, 98, 105–6, 110
medical waivers, 78
meetings: morning meetings, 128; punctuality/timeliness and respect for others, 10–11; tactical briefs, 133
mentors, 141, 148, 156
message traffic, 133
"minoring on the minor issues," 138
misconduct and punishment, 80, 91
mistakes, avoiding and minimizing, 1
morale, welfare, and recreation (MWR) program, 45, 150–51
morning colors, 34
morning meetings, 128
motivation, intellect, and personal example, 160–62
movies, 183
moving process and resources, 119, 172–73
MyPay website, 62–63, 118, 175

national anthem and colors, 33–34
Naval Courtesies, Customs, and Traditions, 31
naval flight officers (NFOs), 100
Naval Postgraduate School (NPS), 66, 104, 108
Naval Reserve Officers Training Corps (NROTC), 20
naval schools. *See* schools, naval
Naval War College, 66, 108, 165
Navy, U.S.: birth of, 163–64; core values of, 9, 69–71; cultural touchstones of, 9–13; history of, 163–70; integrity and values of, 69–71, 83; meritocracy of, 2; mission, goals and direction policy documents, 71–72; mission first, and Sailors always, 83; mission of, 11–12; operational fighting force role of, 5; success in, 1–2; website of, 72, 173
Navy and Marine Corps Awards Manual, 92, 93
Navy Birthday Ball, 115–16
Navy Personnel Command (NPC), 81, 96–97, 107–8, 171–72
Navy Reserve, 102
Navy Safety Center, 59
Navy Spouse's Guide (Stavridis), 112, 113, 118–19
Navy Standard Integrated Personnel System (NSIPS), 52
Navy–Marine Corps Relief Society, 58, 64, 83
New Maritime Strategy, 72
news and entertainment websites, service-related, 173–74
Nimitz, Chester, 168
nonjudicial punishment (NJP), 91
Nurse Corps, 105–6
nutrition, 79

oceanography special duty assignment officers, 97, 103, 110
officer data card (ODC), 109
Officer Development School, 105–6
officer of the deck (OOD), 20–21, 23, 25–26, 33, 160–61
officer service record (OSR), 109
officers: calling on senior officers, 39–40; fraternization policy, 75; managing up, 134; performance expectations and traits, 10, 107–9; relationship protocol and traditions, 26–29, 130; seniors, interacting with, 35; social and personal conduct of, 46–47; traits valued in the Navy and organizations, 1–2, 107
officers' call, 128
official calls, 39–40
official military personnel file (OMPF), 109
ombudsman, command, 58, 76–77, 118
operational commands: bunk and locker assignments, 22; checking on board, 20–21; early starting times and twenty-four hour workdays, 9; family visits to, 120; first day in, 20–22; leave requests and approval in, 57; outreach to new crewmembers, 18; pace of activity in,

15; reporting to and how to get to, 19–20; uniform for reporting to, 21; warfighting and operational competence focus, 5; watchstanding responsibilities in, 25–26
operations: combat readiness and execution, 161; message traffic about, 133; support for as mission of Navy, 11–12
OPNAV tours, 107–8
orders, 16, 17, 146–47
organization: chain of command, 25–26; command/organizational climate, 10; naval school chain of command, 140–42; relationship protocol and traditions, 26–29
orientation session, 22
outline exchange, 143

parenthood and pregnancy, 81–82
passion, 159
paternity leave policy, 82
pay: assistance for problems with, 63; disbursement of, 60; management of on MyPay website, 62–63, 118, 175; taxable and nontaxable portions, 62
pay types: allowances, 61, 62; basic, 60–61; bonus, 61–62; special, 61
peacetime innovation, 165–67, 169
Pentagon tours, 107–8
perfection getting in the way of good, 138
performance evaluations, 90–91, 93, 107
performance summary record (PSR), 109
Perry, Oliver Hazard, 164
personal life, getting organized before first assignment, 15
personal readiness, 77–79
personal time, 154–55
personnel qualification standards (PDS), 22–23
personnel support detachment (PSD), 54, 61, 63
phone calls/voice communications, 120, 121
physical fitness assessment (PFA), 78–79
physical readiness, 78–79
physical readiness test (PRT), 78–79
pilots, 100, 110
plan of the day (POD), 155
planning: basics of naval planning, 8; goal achievement through plans, 153; hope is not a plan, 7; learning planning and preparation skills, 7–8; plan of action and milestones (POA&M), 135–36; time requirement for, 8
point paper, 87–88
port briefs about foreign customs, 40
Porter, David (Civil War), 165
Porter, David (War of 1812), 164
pregnant servicewomen, 78, 81–82
Proceedings (U.S. Naval Institute), 72, 182
professional development: attendance at briefs, 133; CNO Professional Reading Program, 172, 177–82; education and, 139–40, 151; performance evaluations, 90–91, 107; website resources, 172
programs: assessments review, 130–31; check sheets for management of, 136; definition and examples of, 130; divisional-level collateral duties, 129–30; documentation requirements, 131; instructions and publications that govern, 131; management of, 130–31; quality review of, 138; successful management of, 131
promotion: community and Pentagon tours and, 107–8; fair but competitive system for, 96; FITREP accuracy, 109; promotion and screening boards, 96–97; service record accuracy and, 108–9; transfer/redesignation board, 101–2, 110
proofreading and writing style, 86–87
public affairs officers (PAOs), 97, 104, 110
punctuality/timeliness and respect for others, 4, 10–11
punishment for UCMJ violation, 91

quality reviews, 137–38
quarterdeck customs, 33

rank insignia, 97
readiness: alcohol and drug abuse and, 80–81; combat readiness, 161; fatigue, sleep, and, 79; importance of personal readiness, 77–78; nutrition and, 79; physical readiness, 78–79; quality reviews, 137–38
reading program, 172, 177–82
Ready Navy, 119
reenlistment ceremonies, 37–38
references. *See* books and references/instructions
relocation process and resources, 119, 172–73

Reserve officers, 102
respect: consideration and respect in social interactions, 41, 46, 50; humility and respect for others, 7; importance of, 1–2; punctuality/timeliness and respect for others, 4, 10–11. *See also* etiquette/social etiquette
restricted line officers, 98, 105–7
retention initiatives, 81
retirement ceremonies, 38
reunions after deployment, 121–22
Richardson, John M., 29, 71–72, 177
Roosevelt, Theodore, 166

Safe Helpline (DoD), 74–75
sailors: awards for, 91–93; credit and praise for, 130; divisional leadership positions and responsibilities, 128–30; fraternization policy, 75; as greatest assets, 161; knowing, understanding, and taking care of, 6–7, 12; opportunities for, leadership focus on, 8; performance evaluations of, 90–91; performance expectations and standards set by officers, 5; personal readiness of, 77–79; professional development of, 6; reenlistment ceremonies, 37–38; relationship protocol and traditions, 26–29, 130; work/life balance and retention initiatives, 81
saluting customs, 32–33, 34, 35
schools, naval: academic practices for success, 142–46; assigned course material, reading, 144; attending school near command, 149; chain of command at, 140–42; college compared to, 140; conduct while attending, 149–50; course critiques, 147; expertise in course matter, 145; extra practice or instruction, 144; fun activities for weekends, 150–51; group projects and study groups, 143; hours of instruction and commute times, 149; importance of taking courses seriously, 139–40; leave or liberty during attendance at, 147–48; living arrangements while attending, 147, 149; night study time, 149; orders to attend, 146–47; outline exchange, 143; physical conditioning during, 150; preparation before course, 145; prerequisites for courses, 145; professional development and, 139–40, 151;

relationships with classmates and instructors, 148; returning to command at end of school day, 149, 150; review of class notes and references after a course, 146; review sessions, 144; security and classified materials, 147; sleep and being well-rested, 150; study time, 144; syllabus review, 143; timely arrival and standby students, 145–46; watchstanding at, 148
screening board, 96–97
SEAL team officer performance expectations and traits, 158–60
seapower strategy document, 72
section leader, 140–41
security awareness briefings, 94
separations and reunions, 121–22
Service Etiquette (Conetsco and Hart), 41
service record, 108–9
Servicemembers Civil Relief Act, 63
Servicemembers' Group Life Insurance (SGLI), 65
sexual assault crisis support helpline, 74–75
sexual assault prevention and response (SAPR) program, 74–75
sexual assault prevention and response (SAPR) victim advocates (VAs), 74–75
sexual assault response coordinator (SARC), 75
sexual harassment policy, 73–74
ship christenings and commissionings, 36–37
ship duty assignments: basic shipboard organization, 25–26; bunk and locker assignments, 22; checking on board, 20–21; duty responsibilities, 25–26; early starting times and twenty-four hour workdays, 9; first day at, 20–22; meal on first day, 22; orientation session on, 22; relationship protocol and traditions, 26–29; reporting to and how to get to first command, 19–20; warfare qualifications, 23; warship officer performance expectations and traits, 160–62; watchstanding responsibilities, 11, 23, 25–26
shore commands: early starting times, 9; first day in, 21, 22; outreach to new crewmembers, 18; pace of activity in, 15; quarterdeck customs, 33; watchstanding and duty responsibilities in, 26

situational awareness, 133
sleep and fatigue, 79, 150
Snodgrass, Guy, 155–58
social activities/events: after-hour protocol, 28; civilian clothing for, 48–49; examples of fun things to do, 45; family days, 120; general socializing and entertaining, 42–43; Hail and Farewell gatherings, 39, 47, 114–15; hosting or organizing an event, 44–45; introductions at, 49; making time for, 155; professional benefits of, 42; spouse participation in, 39, 47, 113, 114–16
social ethics, code of, 50
social etiquette. *See* etiquette/social etiquette
social media, 28–29, 75–76, 173, 174
Space Available (Space-A) travel, 56
Spanish-American War, 166
special duty line officers, 97, 98, 101–4
special warfare officers, 101
sponsor, 16–18, 21, 22, 30
spot checks, maintenance, 137
spouses and families: advice books for, 112; assistance and support for, 67, 76–77; assistance and support websites, 175–76; care plans for dependents, 81; careers for spouses, 113; challenges and rewards for Navy families, 112, 123; communication with, 120–21; emergency planning, 118–19; evolution of spouse roles, 112–13; family and finance information, 118–20; ID cards, 119; leadership roles explanations, 116–18; naval terms definitions, 113–14; pregnancy and parenthood, 81–82; readiness and relocation websites, 172–73; separations and reunions, 121–22; social events participation, 39, 47, 113, 114–16; social outings for spouses, 115; visits to ship/command, 120; work/life balance and retention initiatives, 81
staff corps officers, 98, 110
staff duty assignment officers, 101–4
staff mentors, 141
staterooms, officer, 22
Stockdale, James, 170
strategic policy documents, 71–72
student naval aviators (SNAs), 99–100
submarine officers, 97, 100–101, 102
submarine warfare pin, 23
success in Navy, 1–2

Supply Corps officers, 98, 106
Surface Warfare Officer Graduate Education Voucher, 66
surface warfare officers (SWOs), 97, 98–99, 102, 160–62
surface warfare pin, 23
surface warfare supply corps officer (SWSCO), 106

table manners and meals, 43–44
tactical briefs, 133
tactical preparations and responsibilities, 133
"Taps," 34
teams and teamwork: group projects and study groups at schools, 143; leadership and managing relationships, 158–59; movie examples, 183; performance expectations and traits, 10, 107
temporary additional duty (TAD, TDY), 53–54
terminology for spouses, 113–14
thank-you notes, 47–48
Thrift Savings Plan (TSP), 65–66, 175
time management, 84–85, 125, 152–55
timeliness/punctuality and respect for others, 4, 10–11
tipping, 49
training: about finances, 63–64, 67; first duty assignment training, 3; flight training, 99–100, 110; language training, 104; leadership training, 3, 24
training commands: check-in process, 21; communication with families, 120; first day in, 21; outreach to new crewmembers, 18; pace of activity in, 15; watchstanding and duty responsibilities in, 26
transfer/redesignation board, 101–2, 110
Transient Personnel Unit (TPU), 19, 20
travel: official travel, 53–55; opportunities for, 51, 53; safety considerations related to, 59; Space-A travel, 56; uniforms and civilian clothing for, 54–55; unofficial travel, 55–56
Tricare, 65
trust, 6, 159–60
tuition assistance (TA), 66–67
turnover of responsibilities: completion of, 126–27; letter about, 126–27; note-taking during, 126; questions to ask, 125–26; time allowed for, 125

Uniform Code of Military Justice (UCMJ): alcohol-related incidents violations, 80; punishment for violation of, 91; sexual offenses subject to, 74; violation of, 91

Uniform Regulations, 29

uniforms: change-of-command ceremonies, 36; dress blues, 21, 54; Navy working uniform (NWU), 21, 29–30; poly-wool khakis, 30; reporting to first duty assignment, uniform for, 21; review/inspection of, 138; seagoing officer uniforms, 29–30; shore command officer uniforms, 30; sponsor advice on clothing and other needs, 30; summer whites, 21, 54; traveling in, 54

unrestricted line officers (URLs), 97–104

VA home loan benefit, 67
vehicle safety inspections, 59
Veterans Affairs, Department of, 65
Vietnam War, 169–70
vision statements, 71
visits to ship/command, 120
voice communications, 120, 121
volunteer programs, 82–83
voting assistance program, 82

War of 1812, 164
wardroom etiquette, 22, 34–35
warfare communities: community tours, 107–8; line officers, 97–104; publications and manuals for, 133; switching communities, 110; tactical preparations and responsibilities, 133; transfer/redesignation board, 101–2, 110; websites and blogs, 174

warfare qualifications: achievement of and earning warfare pin, 23; performance expectations and traits, 10

warship officer performance expectations and traits, 160–62

Washington, George, 163–64

Watch Officer's Guide (Stavridis and Girrier), 24

watchstanding: advice on, 24; assignment to watch station, 23, 25–26; culture of, 11–12; fatigue, sleep, and watch schedules, 79, 150; formality on watch, 28; naval school watch duty, 148; PQS for, 11, 23; schedule for, 26; skills for and competence in, 11, 23–24

website resources: career information, 111, 171–72; community sites and blogs, 174–75; Education and Training Placement page, 108; family readiness and relocation, 172–73; family support, 175–76; financial information, 175; MyPay, 62–63, 118, 175; Navy, 72, 173; professional development and education, 172; promotion and screening boards, 97; reading program, 172, 178; Ready Navy, 119; service record management, 109; service-related news and entertainment, 173–74; validity of online resources, 171

wetting down, 43, 115
work center supervisor (WCS), 129
working environment/workplace policies, 72–75
working hard and success, 1–2
work/life balance and retention initiatives, 81
World War I, 166
World War II, 167–69
writing style and proofreading, 86–87

zone inspections, 138
Zumwalt, Elmo, 170

About the Author

Fred Kacher is an active-duty naval officer who has deployed multiple times at sea and commanded USS *Stockdale* and Destroyer Squadron 7. An author of numerous articles on naval leadership and management, he has also served ashore at the White House and the Pentagon.

The Naval Institute Press is the book-publishing arm of the U.S. Naval Institute, a private, nonprofit, membership society for sea service professionals and others who share an interest in naval and maritime affairs. Established in 1873 at the U.S. Naval Academy in Annapolis, Maryland, where its offices remain today, the Naval Institute has members worldwide.

Members of the Naval Institute support the education programs of the society and receive the influential monthly magazine *Proceedings* or the colorful bimonthly magazine *Naval History* and discounts on fine nautical prints and on ship and aircraft photos. They also have access to the transcripts of the Institute's Oral History Program and get discounted admission to any of the Institute-sponsored seminars offered around the country.

The Naval Institute's book-publishing program, begun in 1898 with basic guides to naval practices, has broadened its scope to include books of more general interest. Now the Naval Institute Press publishes about seventy titles each year, ranging from how-to books on boating and navigation to battle histories, biographies, ship and aircraft guides, and novels. Institute members receive significant discounts on the Press's more than eight hundred books in print.

Full-time students are eligible for special half-price membership rates. Life memberships are also available.

For a free catalog describing Naval Institute Press books currently available, and for further information about joining the U.S. Naval Institute, please write to:

> Member Services
> **U.S. NAVAL INSTITUTE**
> 291 Wood Road
> Annapolis, MD 21402-5034
> Telephone: (800) 233-8764
> Fax: (410) 571-1703
> Web address: www.usni.org